Magic is Real

How to Create Reality, Manifest Miracles and Make Spirituality Fun Again!

(Book 1 of 7)

David Solomon

Contents

Introduction 1

1. Your Magical Abilities 8

2. Epic Sorcerer Battle 16

3. Inspirational Manifesto 29

4 Magical Psychology 35

5. Foundations of Your Magical Practice 50

6 Reverence and Manifestation 81

7 Components of your Ego 88

8 Memory, Timelines and Parallel Realities 96

9 I Am Awareness 105

10 How to Feel Your Chi 112

11 A Miraculous Healing 133

12. Faith 143

13 The Future of Magic 157

Acknowledgements 208

About The Author 213

Disclaimer and Copyright

This book contain works of fiction. Names, characters, places, and incidents either are products of the author's imagination or are used fictitiously. Any resemblance to actual persons, living or dead, events, or locales is entirely coincidental.

In the case of nonfictional elements, names and places are either used with permission, or changed wherever possible.

This book is not intended to serve as any form of legal or medical advice. Always consult the appropriate professionals before practicing any techniques that are contained herein that may affect your health.

The author's intent is only to provide general information to support you on your path of joyful well-being. If you use any of the information in this book, the author and publisher assume no responsibility for your actions.

This is a work of nonfiction, with the exception of the transmissions in Chapter 2, *Epic Sorcerer Battle*, which serves as a preview of the upcoming book *Battle Magic*.

Note that all beings seeking to use this material to induce fear, entropy, and evil are forever stripped of their abilities and bound to not comprehend these teachings in a meaningful way. This statement is holographically true for all material provided by and through David Solomon.

Also note that the author has great respect for Biblical and Abrahamic religions and practitioners, and that the words and purposes of "Magic" in these texts carry a different definition than the traditional meaning.

The purpose of this text is to help readers find and connect with their inner divinity in an authentic way.

All rights reserved.

Copyright © 2018 David Solomon

ISBN-13: 978-17327543-1-7

Introduction

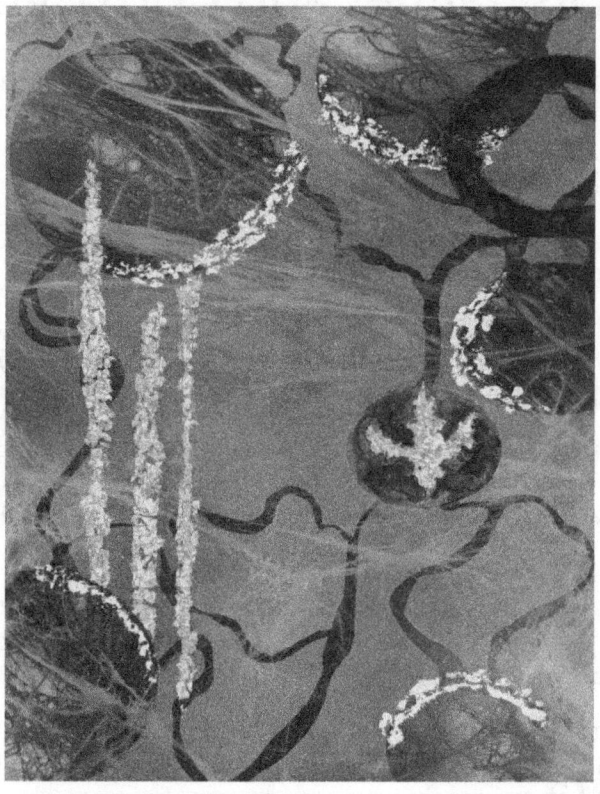

I gratefully channeled Magic is Real to accelerate your path, to inspire you, and to provide a foundation for your rational mind to escape the locked perceptions that reality is fixed and unalterable.

Because reality is absolutely your plaything.

To alter it, to apply the science most people don't fully understand yet (which, by Clarke's definition, is Magic) you must build foundations and practice skills. You must combine reading with doing.

You must remember that Magic is like calculus or doing triple backflips off a diving board: the more you train, the more you develop.

Maybe you seek enlightenment. Maybe you seek more power to change your current experience. Maybe you simply seek more love and connection, and the knowledge to create a better world.

What is the key to unlock life's treasure chest, the vehicle that transports the present you to your ideal future self—the self of your greatest vision, who lives **your fully aligned purpose** and is achieving your most important goals?

How do you remember the true nature of Magic and fully experience it, uninhibited, unrestricted?

How do you travel from here to there?

This book is your key, if you allow it to be.

These pages teach and transmit an integrative model of Magic, blending Western and Eastern traditions with a grounded approach to spirituality that is not attached to any religion or method of cultural control. It will help you separate what is practical and useful from what is fantasy and science fiction, so you can use your time more effectively.

Magic is simply the natural result of recognizing that you create your reality, as you are reality, creating itself. You are the dance and the dancer, the seer and the seen.

This is about remembering how to exercise yourself as both the universe and the will that controls it.

Nondual states of perception—Unity Consciousness—is existing as a Master of Magic. Until we understand that not just intellectually but also in an embodied sense, we experience life as personalities, as bodies and minds.

As our awareness grows, our Magic flows.

I firmly believe that using mystical abilities is our birthright. While they are not the ultimate destination, becoming an effective Magician is an empowering step towards becoming fully and utterly convinced that you are an immortal soul with a divine spark...that you are, quite literally at higher states of awareness, all that is.

With every miracle, every synchronicity and altered probability, you remember.

My past self-wanted just the miracles, the Flashy Magic. I wanted to have rays of light to shoot from my hands, move objects with my mind, heal wounds instantly, and affect the weather. That self-wanted to experience legitimate psychic phenomena and travel astrally as a soul, flying through space, time, and dimensions.

And all of these things I have experienced.

All of these things I teach, directly and indirectly.

And all of these things are stepping stones, just like you learn to walk before you can run.

Before you can fly.

With each phenomenon--every time our intention affects the world in undeniable ways--our ego-mind surrenders, just a little bit more. It remembers, in those moments, that it is merely a caretaker, a steward.

Some say that Flashy Magic isn't necessary or important...you know in your own heart what you need to lead you to liberation. You know which conditions your mind believes must be met before it surrenders the old material-reductionist view and evolves.

At some point when those conditions are met, we start to answer some of the greater questions of consciousness. What is enlightenment? What freedoms arise from it? How can it be experienced?

Some of us seek liberation in caves. Some through service; some through study.

If you have chosen to be of service, to take the product of your spiritual evolution—yourself—and not live in a cave, isolated from the mainstream world... if you have chosen to be part of human civilization, to experience it, to better it, then Magic is one of your greatest assets.

And if you are one of these people, the liberation of enlightenment is just another stepping stone.

Enlightenment is a continuum. You are always on it, ascending or descending. There are also moments of Awakening that when crossed, stay with you forever. One purpose of this book is to facilitate those moments, to activate you and give you the shift you have been waiting for.

Drafts of this book have given many readers goosebumps.

As Chapter 1 outlines and Chapter 5 describes in more detail, your state of awareness determines how quickly you can change reality. If you only work with the material world, your progress is slowest. If you can work on the Astral-Energetic (4th dimension), you can achieve more, faster. The same is true for the Causal-Karmic dimension (5th) and so on...until your Magic strengthens to hopping timelines faster than a 20th Century Wizard could speak an incantation.

While many enlightened teachers say that everything exists in divine perfection and nothing need be done, if you have chosen to live a life of activity, of service, of improving the world as you know you can...then you know you have chosen a life of action, at least for now.

Some practical values of Magic include:

- The rapid and instant healing of wounds
- The benefits of clairvoyance and psychic abilities
- The freedom to experience any emotion at any intensity, at any time (or none at all)
- The ability to receive knowledge from sources beyond the ego-mind
- The art of Manifestation, and how to accelerate it

And of course, the deep embodied knowledge that you create your experience, and have the option to change it in unlimited ways.

In Chapters 3, 4, 7 and 9, the tools to level up your Magical Psychology exist with many exercises of emotional transmutation.

In chapters 6 and 8, you'll learn more specifically how to jump timelines and improve your abilities at manifestation.

Chapter 10, How to Feel Your Chi, shares exciting techniques to enable you and almost anyone you meet to truly feel the energy linking material to immaterial.

In Chapter 11, you hear the story of A Miraculous Healing, and if you pay close enough attention, may learn the simple technique to enable this to occur at will, at any time.

Chapter 12 discusses Faith, the ultimate bridge we must cross to fully manifest anything significant.

In Chapter 13, The Future of Magic, we look at plans to build three temples, and a new Atlantis. For Magic to spread and grow stronger in the world, we must study it more deeply and innovate on the world's mystery traditions.

Expanded sections on Manifestation, Channeling, and autobiographical stories of my own Magical experiences are already written and will be released in Book 2. I originally intended for them to be here, along with an anti-bullying spell which was my first major casting, and an ever-growing Magical Glossary. The more my service as a channel grew, the more words arose, and thus the development of a 7-book series to be seen as one complete volume.

A chapter on Validated Miracles is extremely exciting, listing many incidents Flashy Magic which have occurred in various traditions and have been witnessed by multiple credible sources. There is a Science of Magic section as well, with a massive buffet of citations, evidence, experiments, and stories of people like William Bengston, who has repeatedly cured cancer with hands-on healing in Ivy League schools.

Also written is a chapter on Amplifying Magical Power. Just as a responsible Sensei teaches how to fall properly, or punch so as to not truly injure your sparring partner, I have been guided to reserve that chapter for Book 3. By the time it is released, enough

Magicians in Training will have read and applied Books 1 and 2, and through the fields, prepared our human collective for responsible use as Magical abilities become more commonplace.

As Dean Radin once said, "If Magic were ubiquitous, the world would last 30 minutes!"

Reading Magic is Real fully, absorbing it and allowing it to shape you will prepare you to gain the most out of this series. If 1440+ page books were practical, everything would be here... but they are not, and so it is not. What is here is what you need now—thus, like a delicious meal of perfect nutrition without excess—enjoy!

This is the book I wish I had when first beginning my studies. It blends together over 28 years of study and practice, including lessons I've received from over a dozen living masters and many more beings who have transcended their physical bodies.

This is the book you have co-created with me.

The digital and print versions contain Activation Portals in the form of Paintings that are also viewable at MagicalGoldenAge.com. The audio version of this book was recorded in an Epic Wizard's voice, complete with a full soundtrack that feels, quite literally, like a beautiful movie. My goal was to raise the bar for audiobooks; your feedback is always appreciated! Parts of the audio version can be found at YouTube.com/MagicIsReal.

Parts of the audio version can be found at YouTube.com/MagicIsReal.

You are encouraged to experience this book with a tool for taking notes, physically or digitally. You will get much more out of the exercises if you are prepared to do them as you first encounter them, when the content is fresh.

I thank you, and remind you that, as a channeled text, Magic is Real will switch pronouns from "I" to "We" depending on which beings are speaking. Since All is One, this should not matter, though to evolve conventions of language we mix it up. This can also help you make the shift into seeing yourself as the collective, and the collective as all of you.

And we offer you the assurance that if at any point in time something doesn't make sense, or your mind wanders, just keep reading! Like pieces of a puzzle, all will assemble in time.

1
Your Magical Abilities

"The greatest danger for most of us is not that our aim is too high and we miss it, but that it is too low and we reach it."

-Michelangelo

You are a powerful Magician! Your true powers are growing daily, with study and practice, as you remember the truths that resonate deep inside you. You manifested this book to help remind you Who You Are, and everything you can do.

The next stage of your Magical Training is here.

These pages contain everything you will need to unlock a fuller, deeper power. They will remind you, in a new yet familiar way, of your true Divine nature, and the richness of unconditional love.

Within these pages are all the keys to restoring your Belief in Yourself.

You'll learn about the divinity which is you, and how to embody your soul in a tangible, felt sense. Techniques and exercises to heal your physical, mental and emotional bodies exist next to practical and legitimate spells.

You'll learn about manifestation (making things happen) and why **some spells are more effective and efficient than others.**

You'll learn more about intention, consciousness, and good, rational research.

What is a rainbow body? Is immortality possible? What is divine light? How can angels help me? Do I need Psychic Protection? How does reincarnation work? How can I create new spells?

If you've ever wondered those things or more, your *answer behind answers is here*. Not just direct responses - those are easy (and of course included in this series) - but also instructions on how to develop the ability to arrive at the truth behind those questions, and all other questions, as you learn to safely explore the Astral realms, access Akashic records, and learn how to channel.

With karmic permission, you will receive healing and learn how to heal yourself *of literally anything* - because **you create your reality.**

This book is not new-agey, feel-good entertainment. It is a practical guide, specifically formulated to help you remember and re-experience your true nature. While there are several parables, they include direct transmissions, as do the fairy tales that taught Real Magic and thus were strong enough to survive the ages of Information Control by political and religious powers that are quickly losing ground as humanity becomes - as you become - free.

This book will change your life...

If you allow it to.

Freedom is something we embody. It is more than a perspective, *it is a way of living life.*

Have you ever wanted to say something, *do something,* and held back? Felt your true and authentic self ready to burst free - only to be stopped by a lack of courage, or lack of faith?

Fear is the greatest enemy of your training. Fear saps our courage and keeps us focused on the things we don't want to manifest. Paradoxically, in this way, *fear manifests what we don't want to happen.*

This book, if you apply it correctly, will help you shed your fears. Not just to practice Magic in safe, meaningful ways - but also how to **live your truth.**

Deep down inside, have you always wanted to talk a certain way, dress a certain way, live a certain way?

Have you wanted to love certain types of people in certain ways that others didn't approve of?

Have you wanted to eat or move or be a way that felt right, but that didn't meet the approval of other people... especially those that were "supposed" to love and care for you, and have your best interests at heart?

Have you ever sought true friends - sought a tribe - and wondered why conversations felt strangely empty, lacking in substance and depth except on rare moments of deep and true connection?

Let's fix that.

All of it.

Let's imagine a world where *you are clear on your wishes.* Where your higher self is aligned with your desires of your ego. When you know with absolute certainty the difference between what is right for you and your highest self, and what is a compulsion of the ego - something to make you comfortable. Something to escape.

Let's imagine a world where *imagination is actually the bridge between thought and reality - reality you can learn to see through, edit and create.*

Let's imagine a world where experimentally, scientifically, collectively, **we can test it.**

My friend and fellow Magician: all that you have read here is true.

Imagination is the mind's bridge to the Astral plane.

The Astral plane is one step up in complexity - one dimension higher - than our physical, material, 3D plane of existence.

By understanding higher dimensions, how they work, what they enable, you can understand **where Magic comes from**.

You can also understand how ideas that skeptics accept, like the placebo effect and subconscious suggestion, can coexist in a world of divine manifestation that includes things like miracles, materializations, levitation and telekinesis.

In this book, you will receive a map (one of many) about Enlightenment; one viewpoint that is clear, useful and traversable.

You will receive a map towards Fun Spirituality, and to making the miraculous commonplace.

Magic is about self-transformation. It is about shifting into love and service. It isn't all just flashy woo woo.

Yet, the flashy stuff does help us remember. Whether you learn to resurrect a beloved pet or experience more synchronicities - or even simply live life more reverently, more joyfully - you'll hopefully realize that **Magic is just science we don't understand yet.**

Time to start understanding it.

Time to start learning Real Magic.

THE 9D SYSTEM OF MAGIC

The higher your dimensional awareness, the greater your potential for Magical impact.

We are multidimensional beings.

Magic is viewed differently based on how open, experienced and Awake you are:

2D Magic: Symbolic-Representation. How "Lower" instructions empower you to connect with "Higher" realms. (Lower and higher are progress markers, not judgments).

High Magic is more efficient - especially for major changes - but until you have access to it, Lower and Intermediate Magics will be your most powerful because they will work for you.

It's like gymnastics: A running jump could be "Lower," a headstand could be "intermediate," and a backflip could be "higher." The same reference can apply here - both for what you know is possible today, and what will be possible with training.

3D Magic: Physical Time-Space. Psychology, Subconscious, Placebo, Autosuggestion. The material components of Crystals, Essential Oils, and Sound. Sacred Geometry as the bridge between dimensions, the structure of how energy organizes to form physical matter.

4D Magic: Energetic-Astral. Auras, chakras, meridians, souls as clusters of personalities and key memories from past lives. Intro level psychic abilities. Elemental Magic. Polarity, spirits, angels, elves, fairies, memory, third eye opening to see through time and space.

5D Magic: Causal-Karmic. Ripple effects, Rapid Manifestation, theory of Parallel Realities and Timelines. Agreements between souls for specific circumstances - and seeing how these circumstances serve your growth and were your conscious choice.

Wounds as gifts - and a faster way to heal trauma and repressed memories. 5D Magic is a very effective way of reducing suffering and enabling unconditional and unlimited forgiveness.

6D Magic: Blessed Demi-God(dess). The science of Blessing, and how it differs from Energy. Clearer maps of multiple realities and timelines and how to access them; simultaneous bodies and minds as your consciousness can travel between for rapid shifts in physical form, personality or circumstances. Ascension.

7D Magic: Divine Magic. Interacting With, Requesting From, and (re)Becoming Divinity. Invocation, Evocation, "I AM". Embodied and simultaneous awareness of multiple lifetimes with present-tense awareness.

8D Magic: Perceptions of Unity. Intro to nonduality. Everything, Nothing, Alpha, Omega. All and Void. White holes that provide matter and black holes that absorb it.

A shift from "Creating" or "Changing" to seeing your desire as existing in an infinite multiverse of all simultaneous possibilities, and seeing your intent as already present, then shifting your consciousness to a point of knowing and experiencing rapid manifestation.

9D Magic: Unity: From the Unity Point of all things, this level is simultaneously 1D Magic. At the moment of Unity, your intent simply is. There is no striving, no effort. Often, most lower work is in preparation for a single sliver of time, a specific instant where, like a light switch, you go from un-manifested to manifested.

The Big Bang was such an event.

And, from some vantage point, remember that the Big Bang can be represented just on the 3rd Dimension, which means there may have been a divine intelligence (7th) who offered the blessing (6th) of her exhalation to cause (5th) the energies (4th) and forms (3rd) of galaxies to exist (2nd).

And then, after his four hundred billion year exhalation, she drew in a breath, and the creator was one with itself (1st).

(A reminder that your infinite and immortal soul has no gender. Pronouns will be interchangeably used to help remember this.)

This system is discussed more deeply in Chapter 5, Foundations of your Magical Practice.

PURPOSE AND MISSION

Magic is Real was channeled to help serve the greater spiritual awakening of humanity by:

1. Teaching some of the greater, and now more accessible, mysteries of what it means to be a soul living in a human body.

2. Tuning into the joy many of us feel about real Magic: Psychic Abilities, Energy Healing, Channeling, Manifestation, Immortality, etc., and describing many of these concepts, and how to access them, to a global audience.

3. Including fun, grounded, practical maps into the multidimensional mysticism of our world: Shamans, Witches, Wizards, Druids, Healers, Angels, Astral entities, star people, Goddesses and Gods, and all sorts of Magical beings. As they are channeled, they define, Explain, and Share, from personal and collective perspectives - thus language shifts from "I" (which is usually the voice of David Solomon) to "We".

4. This book was channeled to unveil some of the paradoxical complexities of the Occult fields with simple language and logic.

5. And it was meant to create something that would serve both veteran seekers and beginners, with many golden nuggets for the advanced student and practitioner.

This is an invitation for you to be part of something bigger than yourself.

This is a hand, extended onto you, to join in the building of Humanity's next Golden Age.

2

Epic Sorcerer Battle

"Happiness can be found, even in the darkest of times, if one only remembers to turn on the light."

-Dumbledore

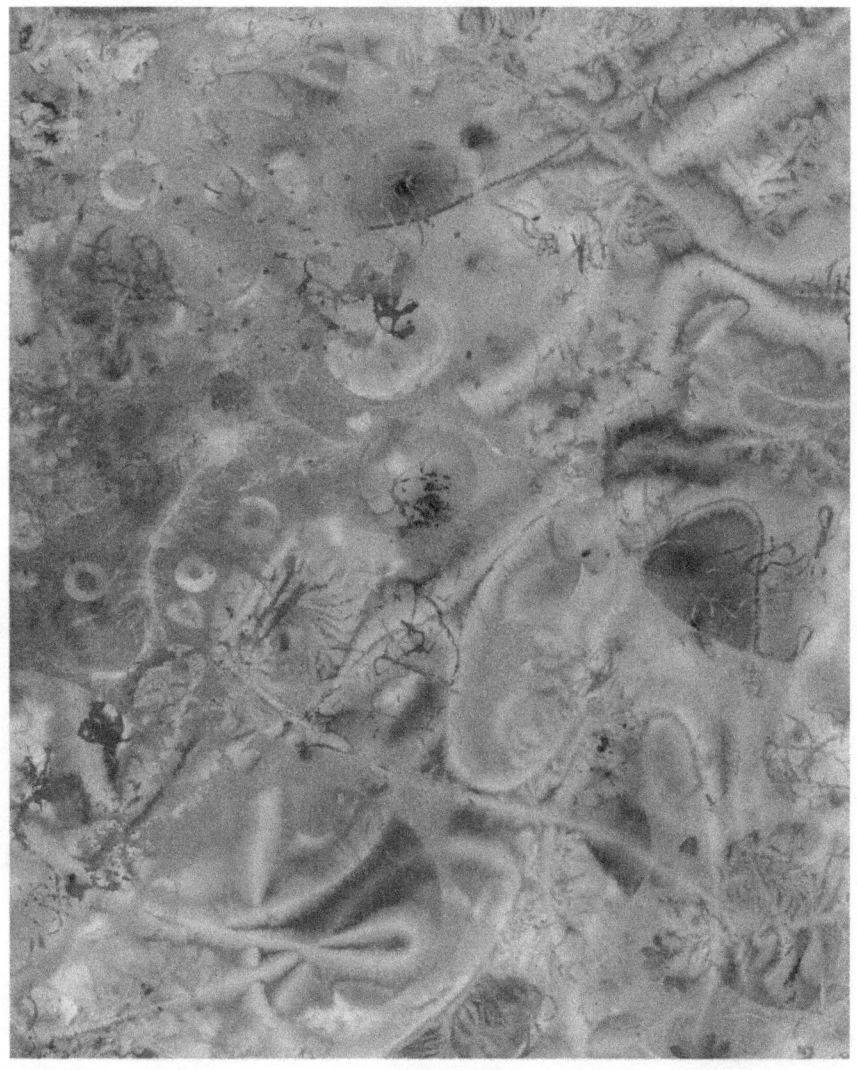

***M**IR is a book of transmission; all other chapters are nonfiction except this, a teaser of our upcoming novel, Magic Battles.*

"Fireball on your enchanted grizzly bears!"

"Counterspell!"

"Force of Will your Counter spell!"

"Shrek!"

I was losing.

"I think that's game, Max." I said. He always beat me at Magic.

That's Magic: The Gathering. Not to insinuate there are other things that will come up that use those five letters. Ahhh, *synonyms*.

We were playing the card game in virtual space with our neural implants, while our physical bodies wrestled in the magnetically levitated silver swimming pool. Multitasking was never my strong suit.

"*That's bull* - you're giving up too easily," he said.

I wasn't.
"The thing about Magic," he says to me, "Is you have to want to win. You have to think about your deck so thoroughly—is it going to be 60 cards, 61, or heaven forbid, 62 or greater?"

He was really passionate.

As Max drawled on about the nuances of mastering the art of a middle school boys' card game, I silently wondered if he didn't remember why we were playing in the first place.

"Happy birthday," I said.

"—and that's only if you have enough mana to be able to...what?"

"Happy birthday."

"Um, is it my birthday again?"

Max had a rare degenerative disease which required treatment in cryostasis 317 days of the year. He essentially slept long enough for the 3D printers to make him new organs and tissues, and for his body to accept them.

A cure would come, some day. Until then, relative to his awareness, he experienced birthdays 7 times as often as the rest of us.

"Let's go to the park."

"The one on Pan or Hyperion?"

"Pan's been demolished, like they do every year during Saturn's winter. Hyperion it is—unless you want to try Tethys."

"Screw that place! It's really cold."

"It's in space, and they're on a budget. Heating requires a lot of energy."

"So just give them cold fusion again!"

Last time I gave cold fusion to the inhabitants of a human-dominated planet, it wasn't there a week later, and the only survivors were cat ladies and other species who lived indoors so often they weren't exposed to much fallout.

On Hyperion, we went to Chakra Charge Park and prepared to battle.

"What are you using this time?"

"Sixth and First. You?"

"Jeez dude you know when you use your sixth chakra, shit gets crazy."

"Arf."

"*Oy vey...* Okay. Second-fourth-seventh."

Three-chakra combinations were rare, used only by geniuses and fools. Every hour Max was in cryo, he "listened" to a rapidly paced subliminal masterwork—usually on strategy or complex energetic harmonization.

Each additional chakra was an order of magnitude more difficult to control in battle. When you have to make life-or-death decisions on the fly, you want to have as much brain RAM available as possible. Max might be smarter than me, but as of our last calibrations, he only had 1.5% more synaptic density. He didn't tell me which parts of his brain were richer and stronger...but I was starting to figure it out.

"Begin!"

The choral yoga-chant of 34 digital beings echoed off the stadium walls as we each began in meditative preparation.

I should mention that Hyperion Park was most of its undeveloped side. 18 stadiums in an irregular grid—just enough spacing for safety—and the moon's icy composition ensured that if anything got truly out of control, the energy would be converted to heat by the stadium's safety sensors, and sent underground. It would take a true master about a week to build up enough Prana to melt the moon, so battles were capped at 30 minutes."

I breathed. He breathed. Neither of us moved.

His lower belly began tensing during his inhalations, which caused just enough backward pelvic movement. Of course his first move was a fire attack.

I fell into my sixth, closing my eyes, and floated out-of-body about 23 feet up. Regulation spacing between opponents was 50 feet. If I levitated 23 feet vertically, it would clear the harmful effects of most fireballs by an extra safety margin of 3 feet. I just would need something strong enough to hit him from about 55 feet away, given the diagonal of our triangle.

"*Ignis Vakuo!*"

A whirling vortex of fire sprang out from just below his navel, swirling with red and orange glowing embers and reaching out for me at alarming speed. With enough heat, it could suck my Chi right out, leaving me colder than the moon's core.

That's the trouble with using your sixth in battle. It gives the enemy two targets.

My astral body swooshed and dodged, keeping Max's cone of life-sucking fire up and out. I shot little energy darts at him, flying erratically as a grin spread across his face, his cone intensified.

My physical body, meanwhile, took the delightful distraction to summon up enough earth energy to boost my durability and muscle strength. I nuclear-force-rolled like a can of sugar-free red bull on lube, and smashed into his ankles.

"Aahfrikiwhaa-" he screamed, arms flailing to keep from falling.

A free fist. An exposed groin. They soon became friends.

"Three points for Jonas Brink!" the cheerleaders said.

"You suuuuuccccckkk" the jocks jeered, dissing Max and spilling liquor on his groaning and contorted body.

A few dogs ran over, and peed on his face.

"*Ignis ondosi!*" He incinerated everyone with a wave of his hand, forgetting I was there.

A free foot. An exposed groin. How could I resist?

Sixth chakra distractions really are fun.

MAGIC BATTLE, PART DEUX

Alex had me beneath his shoe. Given it was 400 feet long and entirely made of rubber, there wasn't much I could do.

Electricity was my power, this game. Alan was an old friend, subbing in for Max, who had to use the bathroom. There were apparently some things biotechnology still couldn't do. Pity.

Alex's choice of rubber was a perfect Material Deployment to my selection of Electrical Dominance, as exhibited in the X-men nemesis Magneto—as exhibited by Sam (https://goo.gl/Szhck6), who was the Buddha and was not the Buddha, and thus could control electromagnetism.

Electromagnetism was force. It was power. It was awareness of the crackling electric fire that powers electro-chemical and electro-mechanical brains alike. Control EM, and you control humans and AI. You've pretty much won.

Unless

You're stuck under a 400-foot long rubber boot.

"Screw you Alex and your evil bet-everything-on-one-move counter to me even just starting to play this game!"

"Jonas, man. Chill dude. You went for an all-out ability, waging all your Power Chips to start out as like, this God of Electricity. I wanna have fun with you man, but if you seem like a threat, I'm probably gonna preemptive attack."

His boot both prevented my power from radiating out and kept the bulk of it in check, since there was no other way I could preserve the structural integrity of my body without dying.

And thus losing.

Which was worse.

"ALOHOMORA!"

"Uh, what?"

"Just felt like screaming. So can we play more, now?"

"Sure, dude. Pick a new power."

I gave him the finger.

"What's wrong with that?"

I shot him a little neon-turquoise spark, just enough to be visible and ignite the dark gray color of his sole.

He ground his foot. I coughed up blood.

It was going to be a long night.

Magic Missile Potato Cannon

"Sepulaveda dynamo kishanti supremo alakasalazar!"

"Now you're just making stuff up."

"Duck!"

A laser show beamed brilliant lines of pure red and green, night-club style, through semi-transparent apparitions of titanium-white and cobalt-blue.

Each laser emitted one hue
One pulsing night.
The red pierced the blue
A dance of color and light.

My opponent was distracted.

"Agni negatori-sensorium maxima. Agni negatori-sensorium maxima. Agni negatori-" he chanted, trying to cancel out the cacophony of light that was getting so bright, it was getting difficult to discern where one phantasm shape ended, and the other began.

"Agni negatori-sensorium maxima," he said, repeating a hypnotic suggestion and enforcing it with his will. It was a half-spell, half psychology trick to help discern reality from fantasy.

Thing is, we're in a fantasy book. With sci fi. And Magical realism. And some truths mixed in, hidden in plain sight. Fantasy is reality, in this world.

His trick to cancel out the effects of my trick unfortunately had one drawback: it was a test of wills, a game of who had the strongest powers of concentration.

I'm no Dalai Lama, but in my 19 years of meditation, I've learned a thing or two about will. The quieter your mind is, the stronger it gets. And when you have unicorn phantasms galloping towards you at full speed, you have just a bit more stimulus to the mind than normal. When you have a quartet of pegasi flying overhead, circling you, occasionally gracing your presence with glittery equine droppings, you just might flinch, just might dodge, out of sheer reflex.

I was winning.

"Terra fumgo Beltane-torrente, mashar-hara, mashar-duckra!"

The giant duck creature materialized, made of the earth and stone around us. My energies were keeping it together, holding the matter in a compact yet flexible pattern. Strong enough to break bones, supple enough to kiss a baby.

"Hallelujah napalm!"

Rays of white radiance shot down from the heavens, piercing clouds above and leaving evaporated circles in their wake. I stomped on the ground and punched out twice, shooting boulders in the path of the attacks, protecting me and my beautiful earthy duckling. Toph would be proud.

"Mashar-aqua, mashar-duckra!" - and a second duck started to form, created by vortexes of force that sucked humidity from the air. It ran at Max, waddling with great splashes which quickly turned our surroundings into mud.

"Thank you my friend! Vibhinni divertio!"

Max's streams of radiance shifted to converge on the massive duck, which leapt towards him, and the earth duck lurched it's neck forward, tossing an earth-eyeball to block a sole beam that almost fried the duck's butt.

"Diverto maxima! HN split!"

The beams all curved mid-flight, then forked, the remaining eight becoming sixteen.

That abbreviation...

The beams kept falling, but started to flicker, and it might have been a trick of the eye, but some of their sparkle seemed to go away. The water duck plowed onward. It was now about 180 feet away, two-thirds of the distance between us.

He was breathing heavier now, thrusting his hands in his robes, fishing for something. Weak enough to need spell components to keep fighting, eh? This was a good sign.

The duck lurched awkwardly, not to avoid a bolt, but to shift onto its right leg and pivot, bending into a crouch, ready to spring. Water flowed as body mass shifted from torso to legs, enlarging aqueous muscles to prepare for the ultimate pounce.

Max tensed, knowing the spring could come at any moment, and still keeping an eye on the earth duck, which was standing still, surrounded by mud from all the splashing. He pulled his feet out of the gunky stadium floor, two sucking sounds following two ebony leather boots.

The duck sprang.

Max shot it with light-beams.

Steam so thick it could be smoke from a burning chemical factory.

Distraction so solid it almost wasn't gas, as the line-of-sight was almost totally obscured by fog of war.

"Sonas muro, mortem aeinsof!" I shouted, and the sounds of the stadium ceased to exist. My power level was about 23%; I guessed Max's was closer to 5%. He had a big lump towards the left of his robe, though, and that could contain any number of things, including a stash of epi pens full of midichlorians. One time, during a fight, he had a hidden i.v. drip set up. It was technically doping, but if your battle partner didn't find out...

I needed to win this in one strike, or risk untold retribution.*

(No spell components for me - they're like drugs, addictive, a high-interest loan on your Prana . Au Natural all the way, baby.)

"Prithvee Zhentao maaaaarrroooow!" Came my tune. The earth shook, and cats appeared, running all around his legs, cuddling, swatting and biting, cutely.

Seeing all those cats dance in silence as they leapt above the fissures reminded me of that time when the two parts of my earth-duck's beak arose from the round on each side of Max, invisible in the cloud of steam, looking like chunks of rock that were jutting up from below us, splashing mud everywhere, turning cat fur brown.

Max realized what was about to happen right before it did, so performed the only action he could get away with in that half-second, a cantrip to produce catnip.

The cats coalesced.

The duck chomped its maw.

Blood spilled in rivers. Don't ask me about the hairballs.

Muffled sounds came from the center of the duck-mouth-space.

"Do you give up?"

"Mmmhrmmmggrmmmnmmmm!"

"Okay, so yes?"
"Mrrrrmmmmhmmhmmnmm!"

Like I said, don't ask about the hairballs.

In Crock, you either killed your opponent or they gave up. Max died three times in the last hour—twice to me, and once to Alan in a free-for-all on the far edge of the planet. He was probably tired of dying, so I wanted to offer him this rare chance to flee.

Being kind can take so much work, sometimes.

"Last chance! Give up or die!"

Giving up meant you admitted the other player was superior. If you gave up in a game of Crock, you lost 80 points, and the victor gained 80. If you died, you only lost 60, because people can lose by freak accident. Giving up admits that no matter what, you have no other options. Max was 19 points away from his next level up.

I had to kill him.

"Mmhmmrmhmmmm!"

"I really can't understand you. Here, you like fire. How about a nice purple plasma bolt in the face?"

"Mmmhhhhmmnmmmmckhrrrrr" and a couple "clack" sounds, like pool balls smashing together.

Or bones snapping apart. Two more muffled screams indicated he was probably breaking his own bones in a desperate attempt to squirm out. Fat chance.

The second-to-last thing you want in a close battle is your opponent hurting themselves, drawing on their own strength to fuel probably-black-but-possibly-just-charcoal magic. It was now a public service to evacuate his consciousness as quickly as possible, for his good and my own.

I started casting.

Drums, from somewhere.

High-pitched voices, dusty, feral.

"Meow, meow, mraowwow meow! Meow, meow, mararaow meow! Meeeooow meewowowoooowwwoww!"

And a horde of kitten skeletons leapt from the muck. Their petite claws tore into my calves.

Necromancy.

Blood poured down my many scratches. My legs throbbed with holes and slashes.

Blood. Magic.

Was fast. And less dark, but still somewhere on the spectrum.

I'll need to buy a whole lotta karma points to ameliorate this.

Which means it ends now.

My hands, tracing signs of red.
My boots, kicking faces.
The drums beat on.

Five repetitions of "*Sanguinem Chanitim*"
And the spears of crimson
Made from my own essence
Lance out
Between the duck's maws
And the kittens
Fall to dust.

Victory!!

"Drugs drugs drugs yummy drugs drugs drusg want d-drugs durgss drugs!" and he drooled some more.

"...and and and then more hugs hugs hugs more hugs for pugs and love and bliss and harmony and the mommy lizard woman pet queen with the massive fractured spleen in a super limousine feeling happy super-keen dammit where arrrrrrre my mushrooms!?!"

"In your pocket."

"Pocket with a locket near my cockit hehehe sprockit rocket cockit vashoomm my mushrooms yayyy NomNomNommmNommmNommmmmmm. "

I conjured a pacifier with leather straps, sprinkled some sugar on it, and gently placed it in his mouth.

He pulled it out and held it aloft, swimming through the air then stood up abruptly, looking back and down and losing balance and falling backward onto the sofa and twisted around again as if looking for something in the cracks

"Yum yum yum for my bum bum bum can you hey hey hey my friend my good friend do you wanna stick it -"

A finger gesture and the straps wrapped around his head, nestling the pacifier slowly around and then through his lips, slowly snuggling it inside of him, and the words ceased.

Embedded within the toy was something with a soft glow. It pulsed red three times, then shifted into a placid, undulating pink.

His lids went wide... closed slowly, placidly and half-open, as he slowly started humming quietly, a contented smile forming on cheeks.

I read the news.

Max continued to regenerate.

3

Inspirational Manifesto

"There is no justice in the laws of nature, no term for fairness in the equations of motion. The Universe is neither evil, nor good. It simply does not care. The Stars don't care, nor the Sun, or the Sky. But they don't have to! WE care! There IS light in the world, and it is US!"

— *Eliezer Yudkowsky, Harry Potter and the Methods of Rationality*

(A free and most extraordinary book, to be found at hpmor.com and hpmorpodcast.com)

NOW IS THE TIME for we, the Magicians of the world, to come out of our shadowy caves!

THIS IS THE TIPPING POINT you've been waiting for. It's time to rise up, fully become your highest self, and learn the meaning of your true destiny.

Your true purpose.

OUR WORLD IS SO MUCH MORE THAN THE PHYSICAL! There are laws that govern the material world, supersede it, transform it!

You are called to learn the laws that excite you, that inspire you. Learn to go forth and remake your life as you've always wanted it to be.

This incarnation matters. This life matters. Other people matter.

Many are more powerful than one.

Individuals can move mountains. Collectives can change what a mountain is...what it means, and how it manifests in reality.

Love will bring you more joy than any victory. Accomplishments are nothing if you do not love. FEEL what brings you love. SEEK the love you wish to experience. EMBRACE a life rich and complete with love, and open your heart fully, despite the fear.

FEAR IS AN ILLUSION! Pierce it like the truest arrow straight through a hurricane, refusing to stop for the forces of chaos and wind. DO NOT FEAR! DO NOT GIVE IN TO THE VEIL OF MAYA!

Never forget this: You are an immortal soul.

Death cannot hurt you. Pain cannot change you. Worry does not define you!

CHOOSE TO BE DEFINED BY YOUR STRENGTHS.

CHOOSE TO BE DEFINED BY YOUR VISION.

CHOOSE TO ACCEPT YOUR DESTINY!

Every single day, you must choose to wake up empowered. Every single day, you must choose to be your best self. Every single day, you must choose the path that spirals upward, and moves... you towards... your brightest light.

Every single moment, you can be in balance. Burning out is for those who do not understand the value of water, of rest, and of rejuvenation. **See the big picture: the marathon and not the sprint.**

Play the long game.

KNOW THAT YOU ARE BLESSED! The very fact that you are reading these words gives you an advantage over your "past" self!

CEASE IMMEDIATELY all of the behaviors that lower you.

CEASE IMMEDIATELY causing damage to yourself and others.

CEASE IMMEDIATELY pretending to need "Just one more thing" to be the YOU that you wish to be.

All of the causes you can envision—money, time, circumstances, surroundings, support—ALL of these are KARMIC RULES YOU CAN CHANGE IN AN INSTANT.

Who you are and HOW you are is framed by your decisions, NOT by your surroundings.

Do you have a will? Do you have a choice?

Yes.

ACT HOW YOU WOULD WANT YOURSELF TO ACT!

Open your eye and see the masters surrounding you; angels, guides, and role models. Open your eye and see your future self, your higher self, and the self you wish to become.

STAND IN YOUR KNOWING that in a Unity of all things, these beings surround you, smiling at you, supporting you.

Regardless of your physical circumstances, REGARDLESS of your past or your stories, YOU HAVE A CHOICE IN THIS MOMENT and in EVERY moment of now.

Choose.

Create.

Smile.

If you died tomorrow, how would you view the choice you made in this moment?

How would you view the choices you made yesterday? Last week, month and year?

How would you view the choices of how you treat other people? Animals? Your inner child, that which has been and always will be a part of your Whole Self?

Like all deep questions, these words will continue to echo in your mind in different circumstances and different settings, as serves your spiritual evolution.

As these questions return, allow yourself to reflect. Consider, evaluate, choose. Allow yourself to receive all that the universe has to offer. Allow your divine feminine to take in that which serves you, whatever the source. Words, people, circumstances.

Allow your future self, with respect and self-love, to support your current self. Here, now.

YOU are the bootstraps. YOU are the savior. YOU are the Messiah of your own life.

Do not seek from others what you know deep down is already inside you. **Live by the habits that empower you most.**

Every teacher, speaker, and guru, is just a projection of you...a projection to remind you of your true and eternal greatness

Discard your cravings, your feelings of "not enough" and lack, for those who do not show up in your life the way you think they should. Let go, and surrender to the world as it is.

Only then - only with full surrender and acceptance - can you be free.

As you become free of the emotional pull of your desires, you can begin to reframe them as reminders of the things that you already know. Reminders to act in ways you may have forgotten.

FORGIVE YOURSELF for not doing this in the past. Forgive yourself for any time in the eternal now of what your mind calls the future...forgive yourself of your humanity, and your incremental progress.

Every "no" is a fraction of a yes. Every "Failure" is one more element of the education of your success. Every experience you have - and have ever had - is valuable.

Know this, at a soul level. Know it at a causal level, the level of your karma. Remember how, as a soul making decisions before this incarnation began...remember these challenges you gave yourself, these gifts your ego calls wounds.

Remember, and be free.

Happiness is a choice.

Therefore, suffering is also optional.

Your immortal perspective comes from your deep awareness of your living so many lifetimes, of having been here before. This perspective could be 0 to 100% online, or anywhere in between, any moment of now.

Allow yourself to be at peace in the knowing that your feelings, your experiences, and your truth have shaped reality in such a way as to help you remember your truth...and thus, in seeing your truth, in realizing you are a soul, your abilities to see the material world as a school you helped design will liberate your consciousness to recreate that world... recreate this part of the matrix... as serves your highest and best.

ALLOW YOURSELF the full power available to you as a Magical being.

Remember that your power levels are what they are for your OWN PROTECTION.

Just as a rhinoceros could break through a wall of paper effortlessly, there is an aspect of you so mighty as to enable you to transcend anything you perceive as an obstacle with effortless flow.

ELEVATE your discernment of what is an obstacle.

RELAX into the stillness of knowing that love permeates all.

Allow gentleness to guide your decisions lest you act rashly.
And REMEMBER that you are both the rhino and the paper. Do you want to "destroy" the obstacles in your path? Do you want life to attempt to "destroy" you, so you have to "fight back" in return?

Or do you want to harmonize, feel your strong side and your gentle side alike, your fire and your water, and flow in elemental balance?

LIFE IS A DANCE.

You are the dancer and the music!

Allow not an abrasive rhythm to distort your inner peace.

Rather, become the rhythm, see the beauty in what you would otherwise judge with harshness. Feeling the gentleness with an open heart, with the warming rays of true awe and deeply embodied love for the life you get to live.

You can see the goodness in all things, the blooming rose and the toxic waste.

You can see the soul in every being... the saint and the sinner alike...and all those aspects of you.

You can see the lessons we all chose to learn and celebrate our collective gifts as opportunities for growth.

Nothing happens by accident.

4
Magical Psychology

"Quantum theory means that a physical system does not have a single history, but rather has many histories, each associated with a different probability."

–Stephen Hawking

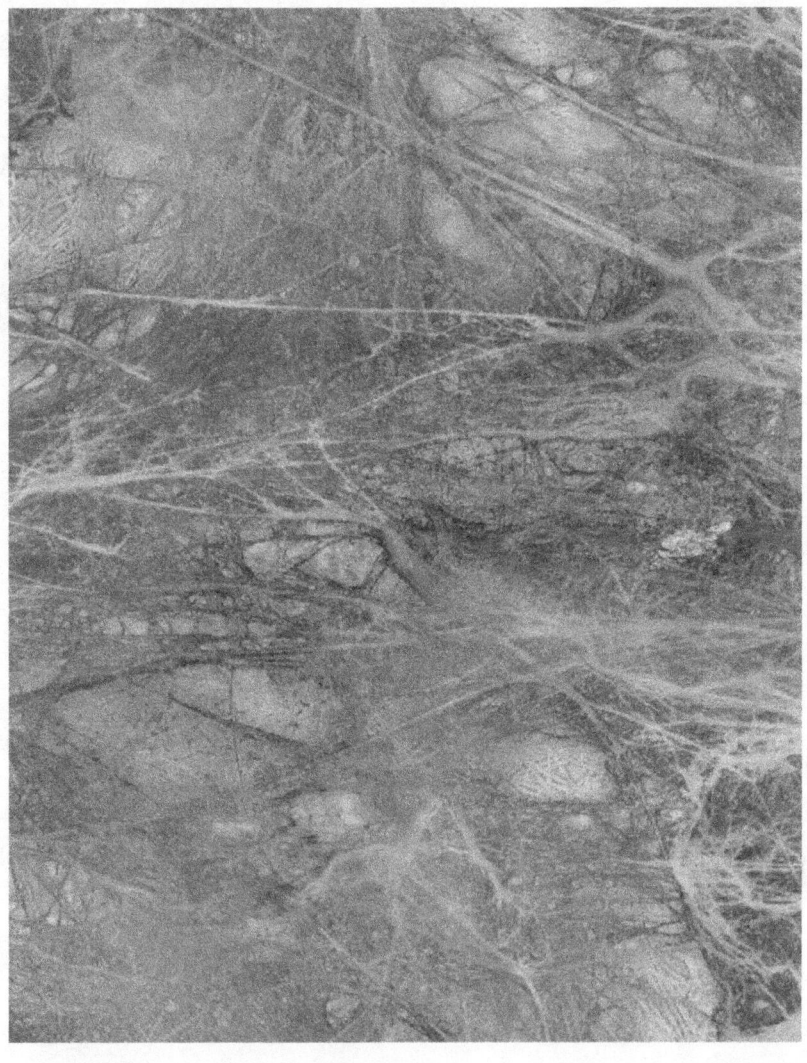

Reality is holographic. You create it. Consciousness is continuously changing the reality you create. Magic is changing yourself in ways that are reflected in the outside world - and thus applying quantum principles to create, and recreate, reality.

Magic is, to honor Arthur C. Clarke, simply science we don't yet fully understand.

As your Magical studies progress, your vocabulary will change. Relatively soon, you could shift from saying "I'm casting a spell to make X happen" to "With intention, X is now Y."

There is no limit to X.

There is no limit to Y.

This book will help you remember that.

And even better... this book will help you embody it.

DEPTH AND BREADTH

The transmissions of Magic is Real will affect your system. This happens automatically and continuously as all words enter your subconscious mind, regardless of how much attention you are paying to the content

Even if you don't consciously understand something while reading it, this book will create puzzle pieces that have their own intelligence and will self-assemble into usable paradigms, given the permission of your higher self.

The more you listen to Magic is Real, the more you strengthen your Magical Muscle Memory.

The density of information here does mean that multiple readings will multiply the value you receive. As more of your Magical Education becomes conscious and fully embodied, more of your waking, rational mind will integrate the principles within.

This will help you shape reality at will, in more and more complex ways, faster and more naturally.

Practice makes perfect.

Just like drinking Kombucha fills you with millions of tiny life forms that strengthen your system as a whole, receiving this transmission will fill your probability field with millions of tiny options - options you can learn to assemble as you reorganize and recreate the factors that make up your entire life.

You are building, my friend, a Magical Neural Net.

YOUR MAGICAL TRIBE

Magic is more powerful in groups, in collectives. If, like many of us, you learn better through action, through discussion, and through live workshops, please reach out digitally.

There are several ways this can happen:

The main portal for updates, lessons and Wizard School is MagicalGoldenAge.com.

Videos will be posted on youtube.com/MagicIsReal, and you can find both images and short videos on instagram.com/SorcererDavid.

A "Sorcerer," in our language is one who works with Source energy. God, the Universe, the Matrix, Reality. All other connotations for the word "Sorcerer" belong to their respective cultures and need not be projected unless you wish the old to define the new.

As you likely choose to celebrate your Truth in every stage of growth - and likely don't change your name at each of those stages - so too, as a civilization, do we need to rise above appearances and give old words new meaning.

Actively participating in online and in-person Magical communities will enable you to receive support, richer content, and more powerful experiences. By receiving the newsletter, for example, you can learn of new group Magical experiments, and how to enroll in Monthly Spells where we'll work with divine beings like:

- Thoth to support your Magical education
- Lakshmi to bring you more energies of Success in your spiritual and financial endeavors
- Vishnu to help you more effortlessly create your reality
- Athena to help you apply the wisdom you learn, and
- Horus to see clearly from your third eye

And many more things like a Magical Mastermind, where you and up to 11 other students can receive live training, perform group rituals, and receive personal support on a weekly and monthly basis.

YOUR MAGICAL EVOLUTION

We offer you this book to help you build awareness, abilities and power as a Magician. Through specific exercises and exposure to transmissions, you level up in the path of Ascension - of Magical Enlightenment.

Often at festivals when David is tuned up and tuned in while speaking directly to someone's soul, people get goosebumps. When he's connected with the highest levels of resonant truth, his fingers start to tingle. Magic - true Magic, effective reality manipulation can be felt in the physical body.

Once you understand now just how, but why Magic works, you will know the infinite source of all Magic is something already inside you...and you will not need other people to give you spells.

You won't need planetary correspondences, colored candles, crystals, or moon phases. You won't need telepathic star people or initiation ceremonies. You won't need a single one of these permission slips, as you will fully belief in yourself.

The Magic you are looking for is simply obscured from your sight. We're here to help you see it.

You're invited to jump around this book in the order that serves your highest excitement. Yet know that each chapter builds upon the prior ones.

As with all things, trust in your truth, your knowing and what brings you joy.

If you're aligned with your intuition or want to play a little Magical game with the universe, flip to a random page that you feel called to. Perhaps ask a question before hand, and see how the universe responds by guiding your hand to the section you allow yourself to be led.

You can do this with any book, and the more you learn how to surrender your ego and allow your all-knowing Highest Self to take control, the more valuable the experience will be.

Every time an adept Sorcerer does this, he finds exactly what he needed in that moment.

Of course, for those who try to force this, they end up faking it - something their heart of hearts knows at the time - and random re-becomes random, losing meaning except in the grasping of a mind.

EATING CHI

An example of this fun test of Magic occurred during the end of the Lucidity Festival in 2018. After several days of offering workshops on enhanced energetic perception and astral sight, an intro to Tantra (or the sacred sexuality and creative energies),

Money Magic and Manifestation, I started packing up my tent. Every workshop was filled beyond capacity, and over 140 people signed up to keep in touch for Magical training.

When all the cafes were closed and my food was packed away, I suddenly became very hungry. The high energy output of the weekend and physical labor of the day triggered a strong psychological response.

This was before my Breatharian initiation, so my first response wasn't to draw in chi. It was to listen to that persistent inner voice, which said, over and over: "*Get more energy from calories.*"

As I considered whether to eat or practice internal qigong, I remembered the *Kybalion*, a primary text of Hermetic studies. It states, quite definitively, that "All is in All."

We are the source. As I've learned in *Autobiography of a Yogi*, and through studying with many living and astral masters, human beings can live completely on source energy. This energy is called Chi in Chinese, Prana in Sanskrit, Mana in Polynesian cultures, bio-field energy in the west, and many other things depending on your context. I use the words interchangeably, one small way of linking Magical systems from all cultures.

After all, if we're working towards a Unified Theory of Magic, it makes sense to honor each part we seek to integrate!

Just like doing backflips, Pranic living is a skill. I recently heard Ray Maor, a teacher of a modern form of adapted and safe Breatharianism, admit to consuming 300-400 calories a day. Rather than try to "force" a system which, when improperly taught, can harm many individuals, he lives in a balance of the astral and physical - with a heavier weight on the astral. He is energetic, healthy and muscular, and honors the material world even as he continuously shifts to higher levels of embodied awareness.

Another friend, Jan Ogden, Shaman of the Institute of Noetic Sciences, said she eats because she enjoyed it. After a very intense experience with Native American spiritual teachers, she learned how to live off the energy of the sun and earth without taking food or water into her body.

Since childhood, I knew deep down that the skill of energetic transmutation can be learned. Michael Monk helped me understand a concept of "Soul Mass," which is one way of looking at how the energy of consciousness coalesces and organizes into physical matter.

I'd read about the Placebo Effect and its effects on the hunger hormone Ghrelin, and performed several experiments years prior where I visualized eating rich chocolate truffles, and witnessed my mouth salivating, my craving sated, and my hunger disappearing.

During that moment at the festival, all this knowledge was swimming through my head, inspiring some reflection.

Can I survive off Chi alone?

Can it replace even a single meal?

While packing under a scorching sun, surrounded by loud electronic music and inhaling a constant stream of dust from trucks traveling on a dirt road, I started to feel physically weak. My mind said my body desired calories, protein, minerals, and other necessities. But, I wanted to learn... to apply, this skill of living off source.

Throughout life, learning this had always been a priority... for the next month, *This moment* was a true test; a circumstance that couldn't be replicated, because it wasn't anticipated.

I stopped to unpack and stayed very still, taking a deep abdominal breath. On queue, my intuition said "Turn to *Autobiography of a Yogi*, in the middle of the third chapter."

I didn't know that book by heart, and it had been about 8 months since the last reading. I didn't remember what the chapter covered, but trusted my intuition; trusted the flow, and did as instructed. Opening Audible, I slid the bar very carefully to the *exact center* of chapter 3.

To paraphrase, this section contained a story by Yogananda of his days in a hermitage, where a swami told him to *"Not ask for food, nor complain of hunger."*

Yogananda—then going by his birth name of Mukunda—said *"But what if I die?"*

"Then... die," the swami replied.

He went on: "How do you think your digestive system works? By the grace of God, like all things. If you are meant to die, you'll die anyway. Learn to master your body if you want to master your soul."

I smiled at the perfection of the moment, then went outside my tent, took a wide stance, and performed 3 minutes of Qigong to draw in the rich, dark red energy of nourishment into my body from the earth.

My hands then raised to the sky, pulling in sparkly silver streams from the heavens.

They swirled around my core, creating tingly feelings that spread all over my body as the yummy restorative Prana flooded into my system like intravenous liquid Magic.

The energy rose up my chest and into my face, forming a smile before I burst with laughter in wild, ecstatic joy.

Muahahaahaa! Magic is real, and it tastes delicious!

Heads turned, and curious expressions coupled with raised eyebrows at the spontaneous laughter. Was I tripping in the middle of the day?

I doubled over, cackling with glee, completely lost to my surroundings.

Food? Bah! I was full of the *source of energy that causes physical matter to exist.* The condensed sunlight, remnants of stars, billions of years compressed and transmuted! This was *life essence* in its rawest, purest form.

THE BIG PICTURE

Members of our tribe sometimes hear that and ask, "Ok, great story, but how do I levitate cats? Shoot fireballs? Summon my true love?"

To be blunt: There's a difference between fantasy Magic and real Magic. I won't waste your time with fantasy, but I will say this: in all good fiction exists a key to truth.

While you might not be able to replicate the effects of C.G.I. with C.H.I., there are advanced practitioners who can light things on fire with Prana - tons of these and other examples of available Superpowers exist on YouTube:

youtube.com/watch?v=wYVdhKVb9WE

youtube.com/watch?v=oEbM_kMz6mE

youtube.com/watch?v=1-YuZHxUXPE

People like Babaji - an ascended master who taught Yogananda's guru's guru - achieved incredible feats of the highest Magic by materializing an entire palace in half a second - literally full of all the rich details of a building that would normally take years to design and build.

Magical power, divine power, is truly unlimited.

Whether you seek feats of dramatic demonstrations, or more subtle achievements that raise your quality of life, remember that we all start somewhere. The self-transformations required along each step of the way are what makes Magic possible...and for some of us, are all the Magic we need.

Consider your motivations. Truly feel them, where they come from, why you do what you do.

If, ultimately, you seek achievement to cover up a hurt, to prove to yourself and others that you're a worthwhile human being with something to offer this world... then inner healing, clarity and belief in yourself might be the most useful Magic you can practice right now.

Think about it. If you learned to shoot fireballs, it would be cool for awhile, but ultimately get boring - or worse, reinforce an inner emptiness that, if healed first, will liberate you to invest your time in areas that truly and deeply matter

THE RIVER OF LIFE

We are one. One people, one civilization. We are linked together astrally, karmically - and at the highest levels, all other souls are reflections of you. The more you offer sincere honor and respect, the more you receive it in turn.

The current of life always flows. This current can carry you upstream or downstream as you evolve or devolve, progress or regress. You can paddle intentionally, or be carried unconsciously.

In this way, streams are frequencies. They are all continuums; there is always a potential for movement... and there is always a potential for stillness, resting at wherever you are, and seeing the perfection of the moment. Sometimes nondoing, simply being, is your best option - especially if you could use more rest in your life.

As above, so below. Reality is a mirror. At a certain point, you flow effortlessly upstream. The same is true in reverse. The point of paddling - of effort - is to get your, as consciousness, to a state where you effortlessly flow towards the river bank - towards the pole - that serve your highest self.

Of High and Low, Alpha and Omega, there are infinite reflections. For the specificity of day-to-day life, you can call these:

Love and Fear

Bliss and Pain

Abundance and Lack

Peace and Suffering

Angelic and Demonic

Selfless and Selfish

Freedom and Enslavement

Sometimes you're on the "good" side of the river, the side that you want.

Sometimes you feel stuck in a current of suffering, or "negativity," and need to work hard to swim upstream.

Sometimes you may have been flowing away from the streams of peace, joy and happiness, and just want to find your way back.

Pause.

Feel.

Awareness.

Every action carries you farther upstream or downstream.

Every decision - including not to decide, which is to maintain the status quo - **aligns you with a frequency.**

If you feel farther from the stream of joy, you may need to receive help or paddle harder, exerting more effort to think joyful thoughts, create joyful experiences, and live in that state.

The more you align with a frequency, the efforts you take to build inertia will create an energy that gains its own momentum. Alignment to that frequency then becomes easier.

Have you ever been in a slump, and after enough time stewing, just decided to do *whatever it took* to get back on track?

The river analogy can serve you well.

Have you ever noticed a vulnerability - to a bad habit, pattern or addiction - and realized you needed more support than your own actions and motivations to keep you on track?

In the river of life, you can always tie yourself to a tree with deep and stable roots. A good friend, an inspiring movie, a restorative place.

Now that you know that this world is more than the material, your options of streams and techniques can grow. You have always known that *someday, it will get better.* Choose now to take on the habits and practices that will make it better, and pause your experience with this book to set a 5 minute timer and complete the following exercise.

MAGICAL LIFE DESIGN

1. Create a list of 3-5 things you want to experience less.
2. Create a list of 3-5 things you want to experience more.
3. For each item on each list, choose one specific action which will shift your life more that course.

Done! Finito! Exquisite!

Often the simple awareness of where we are can help us see the river.

As you outline actions, your subconscious will be aware of circumstances where those actions can take place, and your intuition will remind you to make the right decisions at the right times.

Actions are critical because they represent embodiment. An action takes a decision and brings it into material reality, into physical experience.

Sure, you can practice an entirely mental worldview and plan, schedule and coordinate all of these actions, living in your upper chakras.

But you can also choose to engage your second chakra and trust that all will work out perfectly.

And here we come to the first bend in the river.

How do you feel about the concept of trust - or for that matter, embodiment? Are you comfortable leaving things "up to the universe," or do you need a guarantee, some fixed structure, to ensure life goes a certain way?

How we approach one thing can holographically represent how we approach all things.

Your awareness of any wounds related to trust (likely these wounds are called betrayals) is the first step to healing them. Ultimately, as you learn to trust yourself to live in the way you intend and design, the actions to shift your life will all occur as needed - and practices like the one above will happen automatically, without reminders, aligning you more with a continuously upward spiral.

At a certain point, when you are aligned with love, abundance and service (a most mysterious yet critical element of this world) - when you have crossed the 50% threshold - the river will naturally carry you upstream.

You will be carried more and more in the Great Flow towards heaven, whatever that looks like for you.

SPIRALS AND ONIONS

There may have been moments in your life where you were flowing upstream, succeeding, and progressing effortlessly.

Suddenly, then came a challenge.

How you respond to life in challenging times is how you respond to the river. Do you stay a good person to yourself and to others, and get carried up through "Right Action" one step closer to embodying your divinity?

Or do you take a shortcut, cut a corner, betray your truth in some way? Do you make an excuse, sacrifice the big picture for immediate gratification, and start to travel ever so significantly, ever so slightly... downstream?

Healing is like an onion. You peel off one layer, remove a hurt and receive a gift. You then live life from a deeper level, having more access to yourself, and to the possibilities of creation.

Then, after a time, you notice the next layer. You might feel like history is repeating itself as old feelings resurface - but if you step back and look, you are simply entering a part of a natural, eternal cycle.

Your abilities to detach and let go - to not need life to be a certain way - are what will liberate you from trying to control the river, rather than flow with it.

Sometimes we must shed old parts of ourselves, parts of our life that no longer serve us, in order to step into a new stage. Just like a change of clothes, we can honor the people, places and things that served us at one rung of the onion... as we consider what will serve us best for the next.

The more clear, aligned and empowered you are to this process, the more you align with your deepest truths. The destiny you chose as a soul to experience in this lifetime must be matched by your ego's choice to experience it - including all the prerequisites you believe are necessary.

Whenever in doubt, consider karma. Selfish actions carry you backwards on the river of life. Acts of true and devoted selfless service carry you forward.

You want to be helped? Help others. You want to be given a gift? Give gifts to others. The rules of reality are really quite simple. Even if all you have to give is kindness, the Universe will remember that, and send you back a magnification of those energies based on your sincerity and your prayers.

Yes, the universe knows whether or not you mean it. Yes, you can fake it till you make it. Yes, the strength of your conviction affects how much the karmic system will work in your favor.

FLOW AND ALLOW

In this book, as in life, you can always encounter things that can trigger you. These moments of activation are your tests. Do you respond by pausing, breathing, or considering? Do you respond by loving whatever arises?

Or do you react, get stuck in an emotional pattern, and allow conditioned responses to dominate you, consume you, until an unconscious energy bleeds over into your conversations, your relationships, and your health?

Traditional approaches to spiritual growth can take so much work and effort - until it becomes effortless—it will! For this reason (and just for kicks) we've included much levity, a Halftime Show OF Magical Playtime, Astral Journeys, poetry, corny jokes and casual writing to give you a break.

To add variety. To represent more aspects of the infinite variety of experiences that is Unity. And of course, to Make Spirituality Fun Again!

We see you.

We love you.

And **we am so, so glad you're here.**

Welcome home.

5

Foundations of Your Magical Practice

"Honor your higher self. Live your highest truth in every moment. Be the person you intend to grow into, the person you respect and admire. Allow yourself to be aligned in every moment of now."

-*Perry Michaelson*

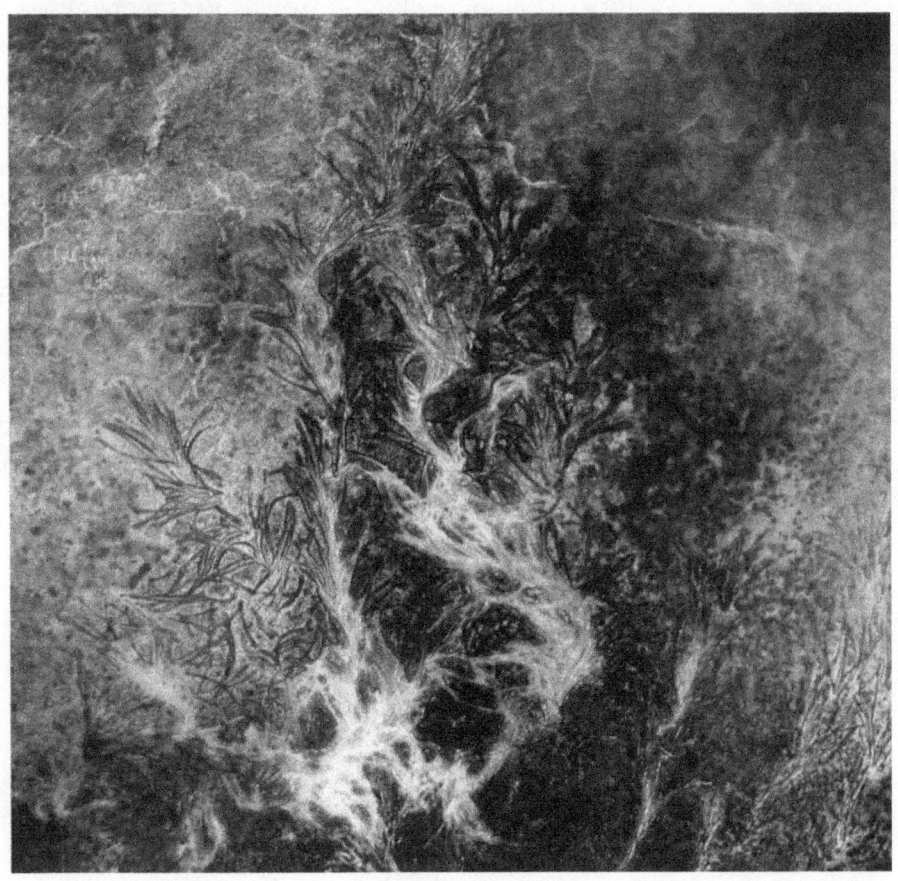

A spiritual venture capitalist near San Francisco once said, "If I want something to happen, I just set an intention for it."

That kind of manifestation ability becomes incrementally more available with practice. Like a duck gliding across a lake, it's a simple description of a complex skill.

For that duck's smooth motion to occur, she has to build up her strength and her skill for years, often unseen, and unappreciated.

You are more complicated than a duck.

Gasp!

Mastering a variety of Magical skills—unless you were born an Archwizard flying on broomsticks and moving mountains with finger snaps—will require a sustained and devoted practice. Just like doing backflips, you can learn how to manifest, heal, and be psychic in a measurable amount of time. Be patient with yourself as you evolve from idea to ability, proficiency, and mastery.

As with gymnastics, there's a period of training where you develop many simultaneous skills, a period of practice, trial and error. The excellence of flowing success occurs once you've done the work.

Certain individuals have been able to embody a channeled skill like Neo in the Matrix, such as Vernon Kitabu Turner in his book, Soul Sword. You might tap into success early on as the universe supports your efforts, as Paulo Coelho shared in The Alchemist— yet the most likely path of skill progression will contain Peaks of ability, Valleys of mistakes and learning, and Plateaus where your abilities remain constant for a time.

The key to proper measurement is average ability over time. Especially if you like to quantify and graph your abilities on a weekly or monthly basis, taking occasional pulses can be very motivating. Of course, just like digging up a newly planted seed to check the progress of a flower, you don't want to evaluate yourself too frequently. Focus on your successes—even the simple ones like learning how to practice! And they will build upon each other.

The following list of foundational skills will help you learn to shape reality like a duck glides across water. You start with the transformation of your perception and inner worlds, and from there, gain ability to shape probabilities, and thus the outer world of physical reality.

For each skill, a literal volume could be written, and a lifetime could be invested in mastery. The brief pointers we offer are meant to be guides for your practice. For any topic you feel the need to invest more time in, consider independent study, or if you are able, a Magical Mastermind where you can review these in greater detail with live instruction and group support.

Note on resources and links: All websites, products, books, and videos referenced in Magic is Real were active at the time of writing. If any recommended content has been changed or removed by its author, consider the practice of letting go, and view this as a sign from the universe to seek what serves you best.

LOVE

Love is a very rich, complex topic. For the purpose of this chapter, we focus on the skill of feeling and generating the frequency of Love on command.

As the 2014 film Interstellar shared, Love is related to Gravity. As the film *The Secret* and its basis book, *The Law of Attraction* taught, **emotions add attractive force to your thoughts.**

Emotion is a core element in manifestation, and true love is the purest, richest emotional energy there is.

Holding love in your system will purify you, restore you, and fill you with incomparable a light and nourishment.

Ideal love is unconditional: not dependent on any person or circumstance, but a vibration you can access anywhere at any time, at any magnitude.

Can you fill yourself with love on command? Draw in the energies of the heart chakra, and radiate them like a star of abundance?

Can others feel your love, see it in your eyes? Have you ever felt the love of another being—especially in a non-romantic way?

For most of us, we feel love only when with a precious pet or person, especially when that being offers us affection. As you learn to tune in to frequencies independent of a 3D origins (people places or things), you will be able to summon and feel love, anywhere, at any time.

If you need an anchor, consider an aspect of divinity you feel close to. Jesus, Krishna, God, Gaia, Aphrodite... an anchor free of emotional attachments, a source abundantly giving, with a capacity to offer love without requirement or limitation.

For further study, see *A Return to Love* by Marianne Williamson.

TRUST

You chose to be born into this body, as a soul.

You chose these experiences to help you grow, as a soul.

So why keep choosing to forget your true nature, and play the Ego game?

Trust is about reconnecting with your deep knowing that everything will be okay. It's about allowing universe to deliver what's best for you while you're on your path to embodying your highest self.

Trusting can be hardest when a major life challenge comes. How can you trust the broken arm, deceased loved one, or major career challenge helps your spiritual mission?

By remembering what's truly important.

If you over identify with your ego, the incidents of this Earth School can provoke emotional reactions that tie you deeper to this temporary mortal identity that was designed to serve you... not the other way around.

Trusting doesn't mean you sit back and let someone whack you with a stick until your face bleeds, "trusting that all is well in the world." It means taking responsible action *while* aligning with the higher reality that everything exist to serve you. Even if you aren't clear on *how* a challenge serves you, on the third dimension alone this Trust perspective will lift your mood, which in turn will reduce stress, help you live longer, and inspire more creative ideas thanks to less cortisol and more serotonin.

Challenges can occasionally match what your ego wants, though during prayer it would be best if you can ask in a reverent way for what would serve you best in the long term, and trust the universe will give you what's ideal.

Imagine, for a second, if you had Aladdin's Lamp without restriction, and got everything you wanted...your world would change very quickly, and your desires—since you could shape reality with impunity—would shape your surroundings.

Now imagine a kind, smart mentor designing rules around the lamp. You can't harm others (wrath), can't eat unlimited sweets (gluttony), can't have mindless sex to fill a love void (lust), etc.

Would that help you or hurt you?

It depends who's asking.

An undeveloped ego, focused on the immediate gratification and believing states of wellbeing come from things outside ourselves, could experience frustration at the limits on the Lamp—especially if the lamp were previously represented as having no limits.

A more mature soul—one who remembers the prioritization of pleasure over fulfillment—might be grateful. Rather than have to use willpower to overcome temptation, the soul could see how the restrictions on the lamp serve his highest good.

The soul would trust, and this would come from knowing.

The practice of manifesting with a "Mindful Lamp" is a mix of prayer and surrender. It's different from having a strong and clear will, where you focus on your intentions with determination and conviction.

Especially when your intuition is still developing, "Trust, but Verify" is an important concept to consider, as blind trust combined with too much detachment can lead some of us to being taken advantage of, and others to release their intentions too soon. While the concept of trust is related to acceptance, it doesn't mean inaction.

To dive deeper into this concept, one of many good sources is the video "The Paradox of Developing Self-Trust" by Leo of Actualized.org, as seen on youtube.com/watch?v=ypSinz7WB3I.

Also great is the TED talk "The Paradox of Choice" by Barry Schwartz, as seen on youtube.com/watch?v=VO6XEQIsCoM. Do you trust the recommendation (or your intuition) enough to decide in this instant whether to watch the video or not?

If unclear, pause now, and go into stillness. You could Google a summary of the video, check its stats, and mentally decide if the time will offer a return on your investment. Or, you could practice tuning into your eternal Knowing, drawing upon your Soul's access to all information through Akasha, and get clear on a "Yes" or a "No," then trust this knowing and take immediate action.

If you decided yes, don't let this sentence distract you! Act now! Use your will!

Another exercise to develop refined intuition is, with any video (although of course videos in this book would plant two trees with one seed...) ask your intuition where in the video you should start watching, and jump to that point. Perhaps it's to an exact second; perhaps you click at a general location on the progress bar and trust your hand to be guided to the appropriate spot.

More advanced still is to maintain contact with your intuition throughout the video, and be open to when it says "stop." Trust, allow, and end the video there. Don't think about what you might be missing. Accept the knowing that you received exactly what you needed—and just like receiving a large meal, it might serve your best interest not to clean the plate.

As with all recommendations in this book, take content as it serves you, rather than a word for word manual on how to literally live your life. You're not a robot, and circumstances change.

Trust your higher self and intuition to accept, reject and customize advice as it suits you. This will help you shift from thought (mind) into knowing (soul).

And if your ego refuses to leave the driver's seat, consider tempting her with the promise of a more successful life, as linked to the ability to delay gratification: https://jamesclear.com/delayed-gratification.

WILL

A strong will helps you stay on course with your intent. Have you decided to not eat processed sugar, but are tempted by it based on your surroundings? The strength of your will is what determines how much effort it takes to overcome the temptation of a desire and stay on track for your intended course of action.

In Magical practices—specifically manifestation—a strong will helps your mind focus on the goal, and your actions necessary to achieve it.

What Buddhists call the Monkey Mind and some in the west call "symptoms of ADHD" is in many ways a lack of will to discipline the mind and keep it focused. This is different from anxiety, which prevents the mind from staying calm.

Many neurological, environmental and biochemical factors can change affect the balance of the brain and mind. While medical data, nutritional reviews, and and healing of emotional blocks can yield significant benefit, one way to strengthen your will without any of those things is the practice of Zen meditation.

Specifically, this means a practice where you are completely still in body and mind.

Any time you feel a compulsion to shift from stillness, bring your attention back to a predetermined point.

For example: Sit with your back straight in a peaceful environment. Focus on breathing deep from your belly. Choose an amount of time, like 20 minutes, for your meditation. If needed, also add a warmup time where you transition from previous activities, perform breathing exercises, and prepare for meditation.

During your session, use your will to resist the urge to move, stretch, or scratch an itch.

If you feel any desires or compulsions to act, use your phone, follow a train of thought, or shift your meditation style, honor those desires by being kind to yourself...and again, bring your attention back to the breath.

Visually, focus on your third eye, or a point in space three inches in front of it.

Physically, if your body persists in asking for attention, you can focus on specific and consistent physical thing, like a dot on paper, or how your belly feels as you breathe deeply in, and out.

Focusing on the dot will help you empty your mind. Focusing on your belly will raise awareness of, and connection to, your body. If you have trouble paying attention, go with the dot. If you have trouble relaxing, focus on your belly.

Infinite variations can exist and you can make a case for reversing these instructions, but especially if you are a beginner in meditation, fewer options are best. Once you are in the habit of a daily practice and notice the benefits, you can expand your knowledge and technique. Sometimes the desire to change technique is simply a manifestation of a grasping mind, and let's face it—the desire to optimize can be everywhere. It's like any other desire... one that is meant to serve you, as a soul.

Zen meditation, if you are not used to it, can be extremely difficult at first as your ego tries to struggle for dominance.

Let it go.

If meditation feels hard, consider adding transition time of a specific length where you sit quietly, allowing any ideas that pop into your head (like when you shower) to be written down by hand—or if you must use your phone, the ideas or to-dos should be recorded by voice, reducing your tendency to look at a screen.

Once you definite and unchangeable transition time is has passed, your meditation time is sacred. Nothing should interrupt it save medical emergencies.

Maintain your practice every single day, without exception. Your ego may offer excuses like "It's Sunday!" "I've worked hard and deserve a break!" "This is no fun!"

See these with levity. Love your ego for wanting to keep you comfortable...and realize that you choose, in every moment, how to shape your training.

Meditation is much easier in groups, and much easier in routine. If you live a modern lifestyle, you might find your most successful meditations occur in the morning, before you check your phone.

If you use your phone for music, consider having it on airplane mode as you sleep—or ideally, use a different device for music, one without messaging or news apps (or at least with those apps hidden and all notifications turned off) so as to serve as a "protective fence" around the playground of temptation.

Choose to listen to something simple and downloaded, and meditate at least twice a day to shift you into the habit as a first responder to stress. Over time, this will shift you away from comfortable procrastinations like food, unmindful use of social networks, and psychoactive substances you don't really need.

RESOURCES:

If You're Too Busy to Meditate, Read This by Peter Bregman of the Harvard Business Review: hbr.org/2012/10/if-youre-too-busy-to-meditate.html

How to build a bigger brain: Study shows that meditation may increase gray matter by Mark Wheeler of the UCLA Newsroom: newsroom.ucla.edu/releases/how-to-build-a-bigger-brain-91273

Calm: Meditation Techniques for Sleep and Stress Reduction: calm.com

Headspace: Meditation and Mindfulness Made Simple: Headspace.com

Muse: The Brain Sensing Headband. *I recommend this highly* if it's within your budget, as it will provide real-time feedback that can help deepen your meditation. If you love Quantified Self approaches to life, Muse will provide a graph of your sessions. ChooseMuse.com

PATIENCE

Patience is allowing life to take its course. Are you more aligned with fire and wind elemental energies, or the slower, richer vibrations of water?

Do you want things immediately, your mind operating at dopamine-altered speeds?

Many mobile apps, frequent porn use, high caffeine consumption, attachments to constant and rapid responses to communication, and mostly anything related to the shortening attention span of our modern digital world can degrade the natural sense of patience that you were born with.

Spending time in the ocean, connecting with the earth, and generally learning to be at peace with the slower pace of the rhythms of natural biological systems can all help restore your patience.

As your patience grows, so too does your appreciation of life. Often, impatience comes from a grasping, a hunger, to have something now. While the Dance of Dopamine can explain impatience in the third dimension, fourth dimensionally impatience is related to the ego's fear of not being satisfied, based on a deeper fear of not being good enough, not having enough, and ultimately a fear of death.

A quick exercise to help you see any resistance in your own system to patience is to pause experiencing this book, and look inward to see if any of the above fears exist in your system.

You could also meet or phone with someone who talks at slower speeds than you. Many elderly citizens—especially in retirement communities—operate more slowly than the "average" working citizen.

Volunteer and be of service. Even though your intentions may be based partially (if not entirely) on an end goal of personal growth by cultivating your patience, you will be creating good karma in the world, and will find a relaxed, reliable environment where you can build this skill.

If we wish to restore balance to our communities, connecting intergenerationally is one very rich way to restore our humanity. Elders almost always have something to teach us, and even if we know (or think we know) more intellectual information, the simple experience of practicing patience is so richly valuable that it is a goal worthy in itself.

(Of course, showing respect and gratitude for those who built our world is also nice, as is doing a good deed for good deed's sake.)

When facing your own impatience and noticing the fears that lurk beneath, ask your guides where those fears come from.

Relax and allow the messages to flow, without being attached to where, what, or how those fears arose. Remember to trust.

Don't try to force techniques or resolutions. Simply witness, and trust that what you need will be revealed in time.

This will help you see how willing your system is to practicing patience both in the short and long term.

INTUITION

A clear and accurate intuition is linked to trust. Your intuition is many things, including:

- The collection of memories of your body and subconscious mind (3rd dimension)
- Energetic information available as you need it (4th)
- The voice of your higher self, soul, Oversoul and guides (5th)
- A telepathic answer to your prayers (6th)
- A divine being supporting you with empathic and telepathic guidance (7th)
- Your innate knowing of Truth (8th and 9th)

When considering the source of an inner voice, knowing the difference between your intuition, egos / sub-personalities, and astral beings is a very subtle skill. It will increase with time and practice, and you would be best served by being gentle with yourself and offering forgiveness any time you discover, usually through hindsight, that the guidance you followed may have come from a mix of sources.

Alain Forget's book *How to Get Out of this World Alive* discusses the concept of Sub-Personalities in great detail. A smart and hilarious FanFiction that has names and qualities to different inner voices is *Harry Potter and the Methods of Rationality*, found at hpmor.com and hpmorpodcast.com.

One of the best ways to develop the discernment and trust of a healthy intuitive relationship is to track cause and effect.

What did your intuition say? What did the voice feel like? Did it have a name? How were the results?

Did the voice feel like soul, which is still, calm and consistent— or was it more of an insisting compulsion, slightly erratic in feeling, and evoked tension in your body? The latter example is more likely something other than intuitive guidance you want to follow, as one of the best ways to know intuition VS non-intuition is how relaxed your body is.

Teal Swan has a great video called "How to Use your Intuition (The Inner Voice) at youtube.com/watch?v=eiiJBfIVmJo.

Deepak Chopra released the video "What is Intuition?" at youtube.com/watch?v=1b-z7N-pExc, and Ray Maor released the video "How to Strengthen your Intuition" at youtube.com/watch?v=QyPaZX_XJ78.

Rudolf Steiner's book *How to Know Higher Worlds: A Modern Path of Initiation* is dense and relatively advanced, and can help you build discernment of higher dimensions and nonphysical beings.

MORE FOUNDATIONAL SKILLS

Your applied will to become a strong Magician determines how much value you get from this book.

Because progress comes from practice and initiative, we have chosen to list the next key foundational qualities rather than give you long elaborations with many resources. Based on your requests on social media, in Masterminds and elsewhere, we will elaborate on these skills and add more techniques and success stories. Additional teachings will be spread throughout future books, videos and speaking engagements.

Trust your intuition to guide you to the categories where you need the most development. When you have live support from an embodied teacher, his will can augment yours and often enable you to progress faster and more deeply. Live support from fellow students can help as well, if they are aligned and there is good organization. We say "embodied" as bodies are necessary for the will mentioned above, which integrates mind and physical practices.

Your teachers need not be embodied to relay other information, of course. As you grow in the skills of soul embodiment and channeling, you can receive the support of an augmented will from a nonphysical teacher.

David once channeled the physical vitality of a 28-year old Arnold Schwarzenegger and needed less personal will of have an intense workout; this skill can be enhanced further to enable a consciousness (or soul pattern) to take more control over your body for the rapid development of skills and refinement of physical technique. However, these practices should be avoided until an embodied and trusted teacher confirms you are proficient at spiritual protection and purification, and have a grounded understanding of how to avoid and manage possession.

Possession is not something to fear (as fear manifests); it is simply a more extreme pole of a continuum that, at the other end, shows symbiosis. You have many small physical entities living in your gut to collectively manifest the microbiome, which makes many of your neurotransmitters. You could say these beings possess you, and since astral realms mirror physical ones...

So it is with a grounded caution we remind you of larger and more powerful beings, in all dimensions, and offer you these additional reasons to strengthen your intuition and will, so you can work with the beings who will serve your light, and avoid those who do not.

- **Absence of Fear:** What can you do to notice your own fears and release them? To face the subject, and while maintaining safety, stand in stillness, acceptance, and love?
- **A good memory:** How is your memory, really? Are there any practices you do, such as consuming drugs or plant medicines, or relying on written information for simple things, that reduce your memory's strength or capacity from what it once was? Do you do most math digitally and allow your brain's analytical skills to atrophy?

How can you improve your memory? What would you do differently?

For educational purposes only (we are not giving health advice), you can consider examine.com, "THE unbiased source on nutrition and supplements," and type in Memory. You will be linked to herbs and other compounds, see in a Human Effect Matrix how effective they are, and find peer reviewed research to see where the data comes from, and how robust and generalizable it is.

Brain Games through apps like Peak and Lumosity can be fun ways to strengthen your memory and keep your brain fit. In transparency, they have received mixed reviews (possibly from reviewers sponsored by the pharma industry). Thus our love of Examine.com's boost to the frequency of "unbiased."

N-back tests (https://en.wikipedia.org/wiki/N-back) have been noted to increase fluid intelligence (https://en.wikipedia.org/wiki/Fluid_and_crystallized_intelligence).

You can also practice memory palace (Method of Loci) techniques taught in *Moonwalking with Einstein: The Art and Science of Remembering Everything* by Joshua Foer.

- **Nondual perception:** This is your ability to be in, see from, and live at Unity Consciousness. "The Science of Enlightenment: How Meditation Works" by Shinzen Young is an excellent book to help you prepare for this. You might also want to consider the film Samadhi: Maya, the Illusion of the Self from Gaia.com and this book's chapter I am Awareness.

Nonduality is tricky for the mind, as in true nonduality or oneness, subject and object disappear, because there is literally no separation. For this reason, our map uses 8th dimensional awareness as perceptions of Unity to be more precise.

- **Rich skill in visualization:** How well can you see, in your mind's eye, the reality you intend to create? How well can you visualize a concept, transform it, and project it into different environments and circumstances?

Two of many good resources out there: https://www.mind-expanding-techniques.net/visualization-exercises.html and http://www.thelawofattraction.com/five-creative-visualization-exercises-to-help-you-find-health-love-and-success/.

- **Orientation towards Service:** How do you feel about serving others? Volunteering your time, offering your attention, and helping people, regardless of what they can do for you?

Because physical reality is a mirror of consciousness, if you want others to serve you, you may want to explore serving others. Even if your motives are somewhat (or entirely) self-serving, practice really does make perfect.

Sometimes looking out for yourself can help you be reasonable with acts of service, and protect you from confusing service with codependent tendencies where you sacrifice your own needs in order to make others happy.

Many beings in the spiritual community have a history of relationships, abusive or otherwise, that led to these tendencies. If this resonated for you, consider the book *Codependent No More: How to Stop Controlling Others and Start Caring for Yourself by Melody Beattie.*

Looking out for your own needs actually does ensure you can be more supportive to others. If you are not used to being of service, consider listing 3-5 things you can do, all in under 10 minutes, to really be there for another person you know could use your help. Provide it in a way they need most, and ask them if you don't know what this is.

As long as acts of service do not conflict with your integrity or truth, they are some of the most empowering, loving and evolving ways to invest your time.

To truly serve, it helps to know *how you serve*. This is addressed many times in Paul Selig's books, starting with *I Am The Word.*

- **Sustained focus and concentration:** This will develop naturally with the advancement of your will, and is highlighted because it is critical in longer rituals, manifestation practices, healing exercises, and lucid dreaming. Prolonged Zen meditation is a great way to build this.

- **A consistent and high quality meditation practice.** Three times the charm! *Wherever You Go, There You Are: Mindfulness Meditation in Everyday Life* by Jon Kabat-Zinn

- **Accurate, validated psychic abilities:** These will be discussed and taught in future books and online, as the category of psychic skills is a very dense one. It requires heightened awareness, protection, purification, discernment, nonattachment and maturity (especially when working with others, such as in readings).

Psychic skills, like all skills, grow on a continuum. They can also be a major source of ego traps, especially once you develop consistent, validated abilities. For these reasons, we have decided to release more extensive psychic training in future books, with the recommendation (and requirement for all initiates) of embodying foundational skills first.

Trance responsibly.

- **Expanded awareness of your other lifetimes:** This occurs naturally with expanded perceptions, and usually parallels the development of psychic skills. It will also be discussed in more depth in future material.

The Afterlife Experiments: Breakthrough Scientific Evidence of Life After Death by Gary Schwarz, and *One Mind* by Larry Dossey will help you accept the concept of past lives if you haven't considered this topic deeply before.

Damanhur offers a course in Past Lives, and during a Q&A with the founder Falco, A 6th grade student named Doran asked "*Why do we not remember our past lives?*"

Falco replied, "I'll give you the example that I always give: imagine that you were Napoleon or Alexander the Great.you remember this, and you are in school with the others... you would feel somewhat uncomfortable putting together these memories!"

Falco goes on to draw a scenario: Imagine you're a factory worker at Tesla, and spontaneously, fully remember a past life where you were Napoleon. If you don't have the spiritual training, access and context, you might drop a heavy piece of equipment and say, "But I am Napoleon, what am I doing here?"

Ultimately, Falco said that if we can't detach from the experiences of past lives, we could end up in a mental hospital—somewhat like the conundrum we see in the series *The Magicians*.

In the episode "A Life in the Day," even though Kady is a legitimate Magician, given the setting of the institution and her required medications, she doesn't have the means to escape. A mental hospital is also visited in the episode "The World in the Walls," where Quentin was under a reality-altering spell where he couldn't perform Magic as usual, and had to escape by confronting his very reality as an illusion.

While the Veil of Maya refers to physical world we live in as an illusion, and many modern theorists including Elon Musk agree that we are very highly probably living in a simulation or hologram, ultimately, as a respectable Chaos Magician once put it, "Reality is what persists when you stop believing in it."

In the same interview, Falco went on to say that "It's important to maintain clear separation between the lives we live." Unlike fiction where everything usually works out in a story created by teams of writers and editors, in real life, our past incarnations are recoverable memories, and visible Magic often depends on the perceptions and beliefs of those around you.

In order to change this reality, we can use the model of a hologram, matrix or illusion and apply the principles of manifestation. Such techniques require a stronger fundamental understanding to master and thus are discussed more in Book 2 under the chapters on Manifestation and Power. We have left them out of this book to ensure your curriculum progresses at a more suitable pace, especially including this book's chapter on Faith.

Suffice to say, we incarnated into these present-day lives to learn certain lessons—and unless you consistently have clear and accurate access to change the karma of yourself and other beings, "breaking" that illusion in front of those who are not ready to shift is, generally, prohibited.

When you naturally ask "prohibited by who," we get into very sensitive territory. As with the Rick and Morty Episode "The Ricks Must Be Crazy," confronting those who can literally create or destroy your world is something to be undertaken very carefully, if at all.

Since all realities exist simultaneously, you can, in theory shift to a level of awareness where you perceive the creation of universes, and see how different holograms are created for different purposes. Some creators may want to be discovered, their creations liberated, and a full ascension to take place.

The opposite can also be true. So we tread with caution, recognizing the rules and safeguards may exist for a purpose. Bending or breaking those rules could have consequences, either based on the rules of the system (drowning) or enforced by the creators of it (turning the power off on a massive open-world video game).

It is of our philosophy and the reality we offer you that this hologram was created to help us learn how to use our divine spark in a safe way. Perhaps in the future, when you are at the level of divinity to create worlds, you will set them up with different rules. Perhaps you will use similar ones. Video game design is especially interesting as a field of study here...as is the phenomenon that the games become less fun when the challenge is removed.

Thusly, most games either restrict or eliminate "God-Mode," like in the early PC shooters where you could have unlimited health and ammo. So we have our container where we can gain abilities, level up in skill, learn through challenge, and, at a certain point, graduate

The Magic that is possible in this world generally depends on your setting. For the reality we co-create, generally healing and synchronicity are the access points. During a health crisis, we can be desperate and open up to new possibilities. Seemingly randomly, a meaningful coincidence can occur—perhaps appearing as a number code, DNA activation, or accurate precognition—and remind us that time and space are merely phenomena of the lower dimensions.

Since we are multi-dimensional beings, with an aspect of ourselves always existing in the divine or 7th dimension, along with the Unity or 9th dimensional planes, we can sometimes perceive time and space as an artist perceives paper.

The artist can use a third dimensional tool like a pencil to edit the paper, which exists on the second dimension, in an infinity of ways.

The soul, as an individual spark of consciousness who lives many lifetimes, can use subtle energy, which exists on the fourth dimension, to affect how the third dimensional body changes, in an infinity of ways.

The Spirit, a term used in Hermetics for greater-than-soul awareness, can operate on the fifth dimensional causal plane to alter karma, or cause and effect. This is an ideal level of Magic to act from as it is generally faster and more powerful. Models of manifestation include emotions in the astral body and actions in the physical body to include the fourth and third dimensions respectively.

A being of divine awareness can, at the seventh dimension, use sixth-dimensional tools we call blessings in ways the soul uses fourth-dimensional "energy" or Prana . This can shift Karma much more quickly, often leading to instant manifestation.

This is similar to the "leveling up in skill" noticed in some energy healers. Certain practitioners believe in many complex skills, words, colors and shapes. Other practitioners simply use white light.

Since white light includes all colors, it can be said to "create the hologram" and work at a sub-causal level. Contrast this to "work the subtle with the subtle" and we see a possible difference of speed and effectiveness.

When your awareness can reach states of perceived nonduality, where you see multiple timelines simultaneously, shifting your awareness to a mind-body incarnation or hologram that has a different quality depends on your level of conviction.

Because other beings are included in reality shifts, you will need to shift their rational minds and often emotions as well if they are to be included in the manifestation. This is one of the basic reasons that High Magic is best performed alone, or in small groups where intentions are united.

Magic enacted with the support of another being who is very close to you, such as a romantic partner, can be even stronger, given the more powerful charge of positive emotions that exist in a shared field of rich love.

At Avatar-level of awareness (where Falco was said to reside at times), we are literally aware of our past, future and parallel lives simultaneously. This is a much higher level of Ascension that does come with seemingly effortless access to Magical abilities which can allow one to "defy the Matrix." The abilities should be paired with a deep understanding of what is karmically appropriate.

Psychological maturity or Growing Up is essential before these types of abilities are taught.

At the Avatar level, we both see and respect the spiritual evolution of those around us. We know their path and what is appropriate for it, and so don't try to "hack the system" but rather simply serve as an instrument of divine will.

How much of that will is *yours* is a theological and ontological question. How do you define yourself, in the Avatar state? By the name of your current life? But your awareness includes multiple lives! By the name of Krishna or another aspect of the divine? But your story is likely different from Krishna's!

This of course is true only from the perspective of the people who know you. If you are fully **in God-mode, you live *all* stories**, as well as experience yourself as the writer of those stories. A highly ascended person who sees this in you, and views you as a being who fully embodies and expresses the divine, will support you holding that frequency, and thus support your ability to manifest miracles.

Thus the controversial idea of praying to another being. If you feel it's easier for you to see someone else as divine than to see yourself as such, and you wish to receive support at the divine level, including blessings and the support to change your karma, this option may appeal to you.

However, our culture has shifted in recent years, and the idea of an "infallible guru" is quickly transitioning. We are seeing ourselves more as a collective, beings who need other beings, all of us re-awakening to our inner divinity, and honoring each other's expressions. This is a preferable method at this time in history for the majority of people living on Earth, and becomes more possible as we integrate the lower chakras, especially the second chakra dealing with relationships.

Of course, as the saying goes, there is room for all things in Unity. There are still many reasons for gurus to serve, both in the traditional and reinvented senses. It is up to each of us to choose who to honor, what to allow, and what we wish to experience.

EXPECTATION AND MANIFESTATION

Thankfully you don't need to *master* all of the fundamentals in this chapter to become a master Magician—unless you think you do.

Which brings us to the first major principle of manifestation:

REALITY CREATION IS AS POWERFUL AS YOU EXPECT IT TO BE.

Not think. Not want.

Expect.

If you're in a role-playing game, you can level up skill sets to be a Wizard, Cleric, Warrior, Thief, Assassin or any number of things. Warriors have higher strength than Clerics; Wizards have higher Magic that Warriors.

The same is true with aspects of your Magical training. Do you only care about becoming a good psychic? Would you rather not focus in any other area unless absolutely necessary?

Whether you continue your training in this lineage or see this book as a stepping stone, *Magic is Real* is built to support a liberal arts education of Magical Studies. Certain topics receive more depth, and every topic herein supports every other.

Learning to Channel can support the visions that aid manifestation. Understanding Faith can reduce the amount of effort it takes to enable a spell to succeed. Learning about Power can amplify your work in any area of almost any system.

As you study the Arts, remember that transmissions of the Mysteries are written with many layers of depth.

Some material is designed test your patience. It will test your drive and initiative. The level of conviction you apply to a lesson will affect how much you gain from it.

The text you've read so far is written casually, lightheartedly. Pop culture friendly.

Not all the text is that way.

Just like Organic Chemistry is a filter for prospective medical students to confirm they actually *want* to be doctors (both to themselves and the system), some of this book is written with density and obscuration, intentionally packaged in writing styles that are more difficult to follow.

While you can always skip over these, they exist to build your faculties and test your convictions.

Muscles grow under resistance.

So too can your mind and soul grow, your awareness sharpen, when actively engaged in overcoming a challenge.

COLLECTIVE MANIFESTATION

If you want to be part of something greater, contribute to a more Magical world—congrats! That's happening right now.

MIR is a global movement to help scientifically understand and teach the Real Magic that exists in this world, and that which can exist through experiment and discovery.

Proceeds from these books and the Solomon School of Sorcery support the funding the founding of Atlantis Reborn, a community of 10 million souls dedicated to full self-realization, spiritual embodiment, enlightenment, and ascension. Using the most advanced spiritual and material sciences, Atlantis Reborn will share her prosperity, wealth of knowledge, and spiritual support for peoples and countries in need. The current target date to break ground is in September, 2041.

A research hub, intergalactic destination, a place for healing, Atlantis Reborn is a gift to the people of Earth to reclaim our former galactic **Golden Age**. Like Damanur, this Atlantis will exist as a federation of communities, where individual cultures can thrive. David Solomon will not seek political leadership, yet offers his services as a channel, guide, and advisor.

CHANNELED VS "WRITTEN" CONTENT

Channeled content can always be considered to arrive through a filter, based on the level of true ego disillusion present during the transmission.

When David releases a channeled transmission, he often says (or is said through him) "Ego filter at 21%," or a similar number.

This percentage is related to language, culture, desire, and the mind's ability to surrender and fully allow any word, intonation, concept or phrase to come through at any moment.

The higher the filter, the greater the distortion. Channeling Thoth with a 11% filter means "This content is 89% Thoth." As for what the other 11% is...well, for the purposes of this book and the rest of his teachings, the filter is, essentially, insignificant.

A filter can exist to convey humility. It can exist to allow customization, and to admit that, if 333 other people channeled the same being with the same topic, there might be some variance.

A true 0% filter would literally "Speak the voice of Thoth." If you organized 10 channels who all allowed the voice of Archangel Michael to flow through them, you could ask them the same questions, and get the same answers...assuming, scientifically, other critical factors were the same.

If in the Michael example the channeling was done in private, then the message's content and delivery might be customized to the private audiences. Or, if Loki's energies were involved in any way, all sorts of tricks could be present...but let's shift to something that matters more:

An actual filter is different than the perceived filter —and thus the perceived ego—of the Channel.

In Harry Potter, Sybill Trelawney's ego left much to be desired, but at least one absolutely pure transmission of channeling came through.

JK Rowling wrote the text so as to indicate that when Trelawney gave prophecy, her filter was at 0%.

Which is why many interpreters of religious text said that *prophets* spoke the literal "Voice of God."

And why there are so many issues with interpretation, translation, and agreement on how to adapt original texts to evolving cultures.

When evaluating information, if you choose to pass judgment, you may wish to notice if you can accurately perceive the extent of *your* filter, and thus the clarity of your own authentic truth.

It goes many ways, after all:

You could perceive someone to be pure and perfect, a 0% filter channel

You could be perceive someone to be deceitful, a 100% filter channel using powerful words and phrases to grab attention... and perhaps invent a religion.

You could perceive someone to be good and spiritually devoted, but cognitively biased based on their childhood, unresolved traumas, or personal agendas, and thus have a *selective filter*, which could be higher with certain topics or in certain audiences.

And of course...you create your own reality. So regardless of how clear the channel *actually* is, if you perceive the message to be inaccurate... then it is inaccurate.

Which is why you can hear the same transmission 100 times and receive 100 different meanings.

Like the mystery schools and Magical texts sprinkled throughout the world, teachers come in many forms, so we have in these pages brought the vibration of many forms to you.

So as a lofty sentence comes to you, freak out ye not! Linguistic styles carry different frequencies, and you'll find a range of silly to serious. The value you are able to obtain from this text will correlate with your openness. Shifts in frequency are designed to poke and prod at many aspects of your being, helping you become aware of your preferences, and your attachments.

What feels true for you is true for you at that moment; just as your view on life has changed since your childhood, your view on this may change as well.

A source, and thus a voice or writing style, can switch mid-chapter. When the text alternates between "I" as the continuously evolving ego-mind of David Solomon, and multiple channeled sources like Archangels, the Galactic Federation, Astral Beings, Ascended Masters, Divine Beings, Higher Self.

Be aware of your perceptions, and your projections.

Like many deep works, **_Magic is Real_ can be read on many levels,** with many simultaneously accurate interpretations. Synonyms exist to support you in customizing this text for yourself. Often, more than one reading—and especially discussion among friends—can unearth deeper mysteries.

Sometimes, you will encounter a puzzle.

Only to find a clue five pages later.

Kind of like life, eh?

MEANING IS CONTEXTUAL

Accuracy is one continuum. How about relatability?

If sex is on your mind, you could interpret a message in a sexual way.

If you're looking for a job, healing from an illness, or at a major life transition and hungry for answers, *your perceptual filter* could alter how you perceive the message. Any message.

The key to a clear transmission and clear reception is validation.

Does the information check out?

Does it match what your rational left brain has encountered in terms of evidence and data?

Does it feel true, hold up under scrutiny, and serve your highest self?

While it's true we can get very philosophical and expand on any of these ideas to show you how literally any communication can serve *any* goal, the main energies to consider here are trust and nourishment.

If you trust the information is true and good, you will feel nourished, intellectually and spiritually. Perhaps emotionally—and if you practice Pranic living, physically as well.

The quirk in the system is *the concept of an emotional block.*

Imagine that all energy, be it Prana, karma or blood, flows through pipes.

If a pipe is blocked, the flow is restricted.

Emotionally, if you have a block, you might not be able to perceive a message fully. If you experienced abuse and it is unresolved, you could have a block affecting your ability to receive love.

If you experienced something traumatic and haven't fully healed or resolved it, the natural intelligence of your system could create a thoughtform (also known as a protector) that can halt, divert, *or even change* the incoming energy so as to support the stability of your system.

For example, if you experienced extreme physical injury in conjunction with a loud and sudden noise (explosion), you might involuntarily jump in response to other loud noises (car horns). This is your thought form protecting you from future damage.

Even if a car horn is not related to a threat, the unprocessed trauma—or karmic / energetic / emotional block—serves to keep you safe, in case *it is dangerous.*

In other words, your perception would be distorted, and you could be said to have a contextual case of post-traumatic stress disorder, or PTSD.

Traumas can occur in all scenarios, not just physically powerful ones. You could have received anger instead of love when you were young, creating an aversion to anger. You could have witnessed a spiritual leader abusing their power, and your perceptions of spiritual leaders might thereafter be distorted by your block. Psychologists would call this a projection (you thinking other spiritual leaders will abuse their power) and, as synonyms and mirrors go, you create the reality—project the light of creation from your core—that matches your karmic filter.

The beauty of feeling sudden emotions, and realizing they aren't logically related to the situation at hand, is that you can identify your blocks, and resolve them.

While of course this can be much more energy and time consuming in practice than it is in conception, it shines a massive floodlight of hope on your ability to perceive the world accurately, and *know truth for truth.*

If anything triggers you or activates emotional responses, or especially a tendency for the mind to wander in certain pages, you might want to pause, meditate, and if you notice the root of the feeling, enjoy the opportunity for self-healing and inner transformation.

A proactive healer might not just wait for you to ask for specific things to be healed. She might know you, ask for permission to "bring stuff up," and intentionally stimulate your blocks so you can notice them and eventually, heal them.

Of course, a good healer would do this at a pace tolerable for your system, that wouldn't overwhelm you, would use modalities and explanations that leave you stronger and more enabled at the end—and a great healer + teacher of full service would teach you how to do what he does that's relevant for you, so, at least with some things, you could heal yourself.

Since books are, three dimensionally, one-way communications, the books of Magic is Real will occasionally contain languages and phrases to move energy through your system in such a way as to help you see your blocks.

When this occurs, please forgive us, and consider how to process the emotion. If you believe this text truly serves your highest good, allow yourself to engage in forgiveness and self-healing.

Due to the nature of linearity (page 1, 2, 3 etc.), we can't write all that you would need for healing, and all that you have requested to learn about magic, in a book that is reproduced and thus physically identical to many people.

We can however offer many techniques and exercises that are globally applicable, and fill the text with additional resources, and so we have.

And we can say, in a way that may be received differently than before, that healing is a prerequisite for many Magics.

And of course... you might not know what needs to be healed or cleared until you actually start moving more energies throughout your system. So we encourage you to *live life fully* and only engage in healing practices when they seem necessary, or proactively smart.

If you are like many people drawn to spirituality, you are sensitive, emotionally as well as energetically.

Allow yourself to love all of your parts, even the vulnerable ones. Don't get caught up in the never-ending quest to feel "healed enough" or "strong enough" to pursue your dreams. Start now—continue now—and accept the fact that life contains constant change. Like an onion, there may always be a layer deeper... and until you're a floating ball of light, accept there may be always be something else to heal. Accept it, and move on.

Everything is as it should be.

6
Reverence and Manifestation

"What is known on our earth as magnetism and electricity is a manifestation of the tetrapolar magnet; we also know that by arbitrarily reversing the polarity we can produce electricity from magnetism and by mechanical means we can again obtain magnetism from electricity.

The transformation of one power into another is an Alchemical or Magical procedure which, in the course of time, became so common that it was no longer considered to be Alchemy or Magic but was attributed to physics."

- Franz Bardone

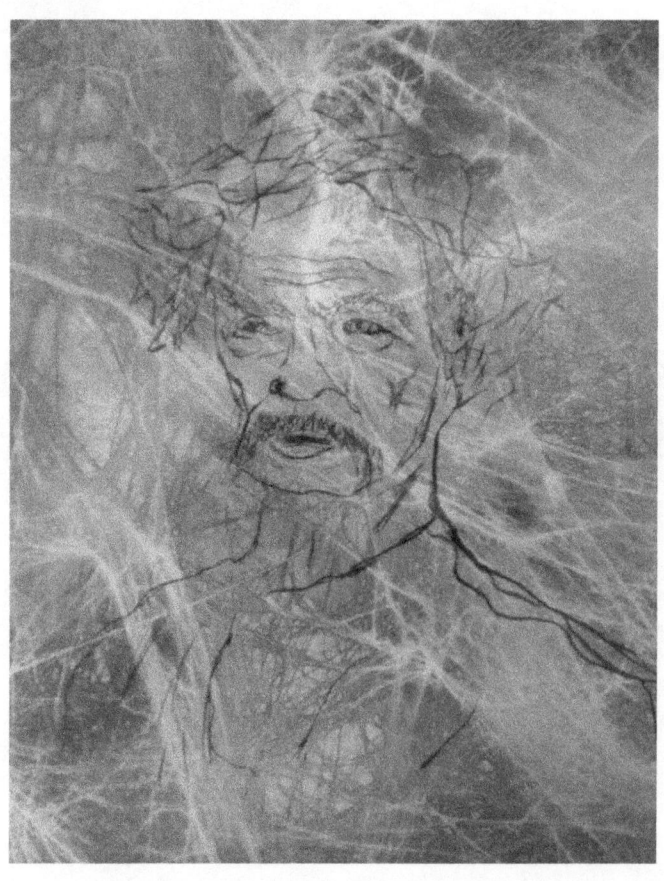

Writing out these questions and answers is a Magical training exercise we invite you to complete:

- Physically writing involves other parts of my brain. The more variety my brain experiences, the more my complexity and intelligence can grow. Based on this, I choose to _____

Your answer here will define how you use this material and how much energy you will invest in your spell work; whether you take notes, and how deeply you engage with the content.

- My greatest wish in experiencing this book is to _____

Let's get clear on our purpose in this co-creation.

- The next spell I will do is _____
- Because I want _____
- Manifesting this will help me feel _____
- And change my life by _____

Consider in rich detail what life will be like when your intentions manifest.

To help anchor this wish and turn it into a Magical act (spell) that will shape your reality (5th), attract the support of loving astral beings (4th) and prime your subconscious mind (3rd) to find what will support you, write out these details of your wish as if it were completely fulfilled. Invest yourself in creating at least 10 sentences of rich detail.

Use the present tense, positive framing. Have *fun*. Aim to only write what feels true and aligned with your highest self. Include what you believe is possible in this life.

As your bar of what is possible grows, so too will the scope, depth and scale of your intentions. This exercise is a beginning practice for reality creation, and one you would benefit from practicing weekly. The more you can visualize with a felt sense of *knowing* your intent as true, the more you actually manifest the details in causal, astral and physical reality.

This exercise will also support the more advanced work in our chapters on Manifestation. A bonus guide on goal setting was also provided with over 22 pages of info and exercises. This will be published in Magic is Real, Book 2.

REVERENCE AND CONNECTION

As a Magician, you cast SPELLS: Super Powerful Energy Liberations + Living Systems. That's Cute Code for **"We choose our own meaning of life for all things, so let's use a fun word that can be synonymous with Prayer, Transmutation, Intention, Magical Action, Manifestation, and Realization."**

MIR may feel both reverent and irreverent. By playing with language, we make it more accessible, and free ourselves from the constructs of "It must be this way."

When talking with a divine being, you could prostrate yourself and talk in formal honorifics of a traditional dialect. You could also just say "Hey Krishna, I so appreciate you. Can you please help me with something?"

Just as with a close friend, intent matters most.

So while I revere, respect and admire Jesus, calling him my friend does nothing to detract from his majesty. Same with Lakshmi, Athena, Apollo, Ganesh and other beings I work with. If anything, casual language makes the relationship more *real*.

Yes, reverence has an effect. But so too does sincerity. Reverence is one of the most powerful ways to honor another being, and thus allow them to honor you, likely by providing the support you need.

Yet if you aren't used to communicating with—or even acknowledging—higher dimensional beings, your greatest expression of reverence may simply be "hello."

Allow your devotion to grow naturally. Don't force it, or it will feel fake. We don't believe things that are fake, and since belief is a prerequisite to expectation, *you must believe in these beings in order for them to help you.*

This choice of freedom of language is also a higher form of respect. In acknowledging higher beings we relax around them and allow ourselves to truly develop a relationship, *communicating with rather than talking at.*

Beings of higher intelligence can understand more complex language. Beings of higher spiritual ability can more clearly read your thoughts and intents, with your permission. Beings of higher love can understand, love and forgive with much more effortless flow than what the average human allows himself to express.

Given this, don't wait to communicate with higher beings. Don't make yourself jump through hoops of cleansing, purification, or worthiness. These actions, along with and especially sincere praise, can strengthen a relationship so long as they are genuine and filled with positive emotion.

If you feel *obligated* to take a ritual bath, atone for a past action in exhaustive ways, or fulfill any other prerequisite that drives you from building a relationship with your divine family... consider just chilling out.

A best friend or close family member who loves and accepts you unconditionally probably won't require these things for a sincere conversation. If you want that type of a bond with spiritual mentors, allow yourself to view them as beings that have the same capacity to be close to you, so you can be close to them.

In Unity, All is One. Rising above all concepts of masters, angels and goddesses for a moment, remember that your ability to sincerely and genuinely *connect* is your ability to *be with* yourself.

As the universe, *Your Wish is Your Command.*

So consider letting go of all the conditions for your wishes to be granted. If that's too much to accept, let go of some conditions.

If it's a busy day and you're just remembering to ask Thoth for Magical help before bed, go for it!

If you're rushing into a negotiation and want to embody more loving kindness, and want to ask Jesus for help, but feel too embarrassed because you're on the toilet and pausing for a minute of sincere connection would literally make you anxious, don't wait! These beings—these aspects of you—are of the highest maturity. And come on, why should we let a little poop get in the way of forgiveness?

Regardless of where your practice starts, consider always leveling it up. If you want to be an Olympian at Magic, and want to have a rich, sincere connection with the divine, then one day it might make sense to offer a deep ritual, with a full purification practice, colored robes, sacred objects and dedications.

Plenty of Magicians around the world operate under those conditions—and plenty of them don't. Whatever you sincerely feel programs the field and shifts you internally is what you should gravitate towards.

And with all seriousness, take that extra minute. Clean up, get quiet, put your hands together, and fully devote yourself to God. Allow her to see you, to feel you, to know you. Open your heart and your mind and pour forth all of your fears, offering them to her to transmute and cleanse.

See the Supreme, the Mighty, the Creator, as a being who truly cares for you. Ask for what you want, and trust in his wisdom to give you what you *need*.

And then, at the end of your prayer, your divine Spell and true moment of connection, let it go. Allow whatever will happen to happen, and appreciate the miracle of being alive.

You've done enough.

UNIVERSALITY

Vocabulary and holy names from many traditions are blended here. All are names of the All. To honor the current cultural custom, I have refrained from using certain representations of Islam, for which I have great respect, the teachings, and the peoples. You of that faith and any other, consider the words, representations, and descriptions of your tradition as interchangeable with the vocabulary of this book, as it feels true in your heart.

May all the original teachings of the original authors of all religions, known and unknown, be seen for their original intent of humanity's spiritual liberation. Let us be free of cultural and political distortion. May all beings feel the abundance and love, and receive divine clarity, living together on this beautiful Earth in harmony.

May we all coexist in peace.

LIGHT AND DARK

The word "darkness" in many Magical traditions does not mean evil. It can refer to a polarity (Hermetics), water energies (Qigong), or hidden knowledge (Psychology).

The Shadow concept of Jungian schools, along with the Christian and Buddhist systems of demonic or "dark" forces can—as with the loaded word *ego*—complicate things. As always, trust your heart if the context isn't clear. Multiple meanings can exist, but in any specific moment, one intent, is supreme.

As you communicate, consider being as clear as you are able. As you receive communication, pause when considering ambiguity, and try to find, in the stillness of your heart, the true meaning amidst a cloud of probabilities. If one meaning is obscured, avoid the trap of overthinking by simply *letting it go*. This will serve you well in your education and your life. Any obfuscations are there for reasons, and if you don't figure something out immediately, set an intention for the meaning to become clear in time. Ask for a sign... *decide on receiving a sign...* and so shall it be.

Death is a transition, and cells in your body die every day. Death is not something to be feared.

Death is a stage of existence, like peeing. It's ordinary, plain, and meaningless unless you so choose to ascribe meaning.

Death is not evil. It is normal.

Evil however, is a separate concept. It shall not be discussed until much later, when we have fortified your system. For now, consider the following practice, given with the intent of enhancing your capacity to embody love, and the intent to serve life.

7
Components of your Ego

"You cannot beat a river into submission. You have to surrender to its current, and use its power as your own."

"I control it by surrendering to control? That doesn't make any sense."

"Not everything does. Not everything has to. Your intellect has taken you far in life, but it will take you no further. Surrender, Stephen. Silence your ego, and your power will rise.

"Come with me."

-Dr Strange

If you don't yet have one, establish a Dedicated Magical Notebook or Grimoire.

Write down one of your most persistent sub-personalities, inner voices, or egos. Describe in ten detailed sentences how it affects you, in ways you desire and ways you don't.

*What does it say?
When does it speak?
Does it offer suggestions or order directions?
What happens when you follow its advice?
Ignore it?
Argue with it?*

*Trust the voice without resistance?
Let the ego speak from your mouth without you* (as the primary awareness) *editing any of the words?
What happens when you suppress this ego and pretend it doesn't exist?
What if you were to let it run free for the rest of your life?
What if it were to entirely disappear?*

The simplest types of egos are the "Angel on one shoulder, Devil on the other." Sometimes they take on the face, voice and vocabulary of someone you know, or respect. Sometimes they take on aspects of fictional characters, or qualities like "the voice of peace" or "the voice of my anger."

Get to know these energies. If you want a huge boost to your self-awareness, take the above questions as a template, and write out answers for every ego you can identify.

You will, eventually, run out. While you can open to the creative energies of the Universe and fill out answers for an unlimited cast of characters, be honest with yourself and only include the egos that show up on a regular basis.

This practice will help you realize... **that you are a collective.**

...
You are a "we".
...

Stylistically, in written communication, those ellipses are the only way to indicate a pause intuitively, connecting with your right brain. If you're listening to the audio version of this book, you'll have experienced a pause in narration. This is, of course, to allow a very significant concept to sink in.

Heart. Lungs. Stomach. These all exist with their own agency—yet with intent, you can exercise your agency over them.

Each has its own intelligence, and because of your superior intelligence and control, you can, most of the time, override the intelligence of the various components of you.

Unify yourself.

Just like practicing breathing techniques can harmonize your heart rate and brain patterns, performing the above exercise can help you *identify and integrate the various aspects of your personality.*

MULTIPLE PERSONALITIES?

In clinical, western psychology, the above exercise could be seen as one to identify Multiple Personality Disorder. Jettison all fear of that concept now.

MPD is a rare condition where certain Egos are extremely developed, and your overriding Self—your primary Awareness—lacks sufficient will to integrate the unique components.

MPD is also on the extreme pole of a continuum. The opposite pole of that continuum is full and complete unity—the integrated self.

It is the self that is and feels whole, even though he expresses himself differently to a lover than to his grandmother.

It is the self that is a soul embodied, being aware of and celebrating multifaceted aspects of one self. This is a state of transcendence from where many of us live, which is a state of trying to control separate personality elements that compete for attention.

If you want to fully integrate a component (or, as mentioned earlier, notice if it's an entity or energy that does not belong in your system), ask where it came from. What it wants. If it wants to be part of you. If it wants to harmonize with you, or completely dominate and take control.

Give it a body (or see the body it already has) in your imagination. Talk with it, give it a name. Run it by a mentor, ideally an embodied one.

EGO DEATH EXERCISE

- *Write out a short story about your life, but as if that ego were fully gone and not present.*

How would you think? Feel? Act?

What would your inner environment be?

How would you treat yourself, and others?

EGO INTEGRATION EXERCISE

Repeat the above, as if you completely integrated that element of yourself. Narrate your life story once you have fully accepted this ego, loved it, allowed it to be fully expressed in safe and healthy ways.

In this story, all of the inhibitions you have felt are removed. All the permission slips are granted. Experiment with fantasy or science fiction elements if this helps; *this is a story, not a plan.* This exercise is also private; **be fully and completely honest with yourself.**

How do you feel?

What do you feel called to do?

The more you realize *from your own experience* that you are the awareness which transcends all ego, the more freedom you have to live a life without limits.

And with this practice comes fewer on your Magical expression.

The above exercises can be supported by genuine Near-Death Experiences, moments of transcendent consciousness, truly mystical experiences, sensory deprivation tanks, and structured, safe and integrated psychedelic journey.

For legal reasons, we can't recommend these journeys, though we have heard of some well-funded, professionally operated, spiritually aligned, well-staffed, scientifically transparent and successful retreat centers in Costa Rica and elsewhere...

We read for inspiration, we practice for progress.

Do you want to practice as you have read, or listened?

Did you do all of the above exercises?

Did you tune into your intuition to see how many egos you would be best served performing these exercises with?

Have you scheduled time—and internally committed to this time—to finish?

UNCONDITIONAL LOVE 101

See every being as a soul. The personalities we wear, the bodies and minds that serve us for a few short years of each incarnation—they are not the true, the complete, us.

You are not your name, your face, your identity, your past. You are an immortal soul, and so is everyone else on this planet.

The conviction that brought you to these pages, the deep knowing that Magic is Real...is not just about flying on broomsticks or teleporting. It's not about shooting sparks out of a wand, getting special powers, seeing into the future, becoming a psychic warrior.

While you may experience some (or perhaps all) of those in this lifetime, what is infinitely more important is your connection to the divine—and the divine in you—which is the basis for all power.

What did hearing those words make you feel?

Frustration at hearing a repeated concept?

Noticing your intentions have changed?

Gratitude or surrender? Resignation?

Bliss?

Quiet, peaceful stillness?

Annoyance?
Are you feeling annoyed?

What is annoyance?

The opportunity.

To know.

Patience.

And in patience

Knowing yourself

Loving yourself

At any moment, at any time

And holding the trust

That deep down, everything is, and will be, okay.

Through the ages, minutes, seconds and moments of your decisions to judge or not to judge, in each of these moments you have the option of ascending a little bit more.

As with ascension, there is also descension. You are on the river of life, and the river is always flowing.

Some egos are higher than others.

Until you transcend the Halls of Amenti as Thoth did in the Emerald Tablets—until you have truly escaped the karmic cycles of death and rebirth—you exist within the flow of current.

Your egos are the rocks that can scrape you as you slip downstream, and the debris you must swim around to move up. They are the trees you can grab onto to hold yourself still, and they are the *need to paddle* and the *reluctance to paddle*.

If you ever get tired, if paddling gets cumbersome... ask for beings of light and love to help. Ask those of service to do what they do.

And you may find

That someone

Throws you a rope.

Do you love yourself, regardless of where you are on the river?

Do you love others, whether you perceive them to be a rock or a tree?

Can you love the rivers, everywhere they have brought you, and everywhere they lead to, no matter the distance?

If you can maintain the knowing that you are a soul, a being above all rivers and all rocks, a being who has taken on and discarded *thousands* of egos through the ages... then your attachment to any one of them, your desires for it to be stronger or weaker, more or less in the spotlight of your life... your attachments will lessen.

And when this happens, when your awareness rises above the mortal existence of a single life and identity... then... loving becomes easier.

Can you be there now?

Can you shift?

Try it. Practice.

It will become easier.

With every intentional effort, with every effortless shift, with each extra second you spend loving all that is in your awareness

It becomes

More and more

Automatic.

I love you.

Do you feel it?

Open.

Receive.

Bathe... in the frequency... that is love.

I love you.

You. Are. Enough

Rest

And be

At peace.

8
Memory, Timelines and Parallel Realities

"When local awareness unhooks from thinking and ego functioning, local awareness has intelligence and intention inherent within it. Thinking is returned to its natural function as the sixth sense; it's no longer the primary way of knowing.

This means that the "doer", from everyday mind, is no longer the actor initiating choice."

- Loch Kelly, Shift Into Freedom: The Science and Practice of Open-Hearted Awareness

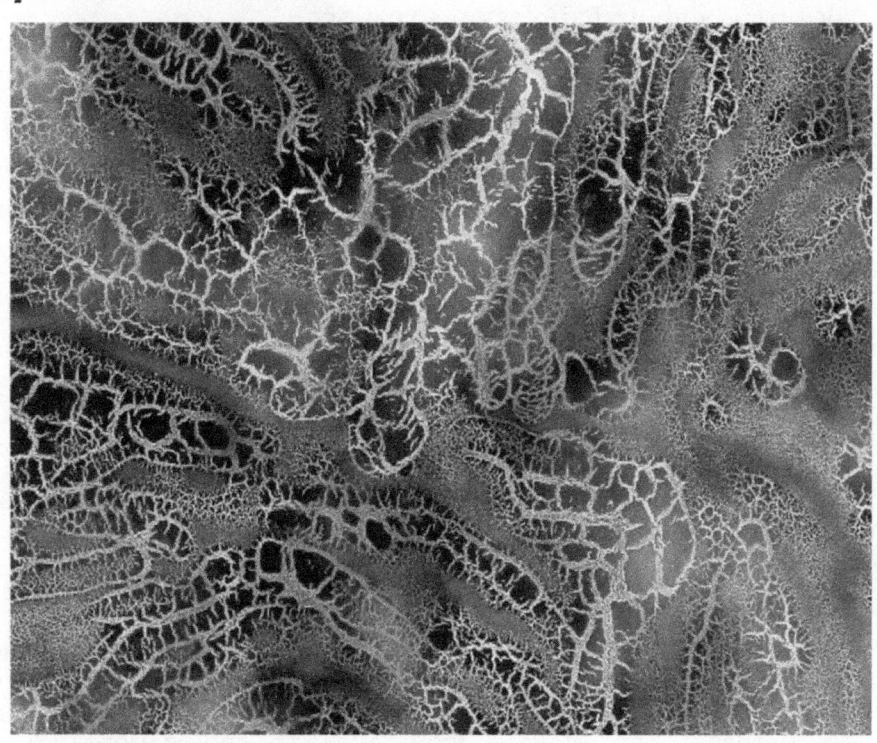

This is your nondual primer, written with tools of duality. When you look into your reflection with another mirror behind you, and see the infinite hall of mirrors, seeing the same image represented countless times in a portal to infinity... you realize.

The hand grasps itself.

The serpent swallows its tail.

Every reading of this chapter is a ride in the vehicle of transmutation, purifying the metal of your spirit as you ascend into gold, into crystal, into light.

This is your chariot to self-realization.

The most powerful and most insignificant of all text, and all points in between, if you see it as such.

Words. Symbols. Expression. Creation.

The observer is the creator. The wave function of Quantum Spirituality collapses, and reality... is.

And based on your perception, your choices, it is also not, always and all ways, as you are free to choose, in every moment herein.

Therefore let this work serve as your Bible or your toilet paper, based on what you need most in this moment.

It is through the strength of your will that you elevate:

**Idea to Thought
Thought to Hope
Hope to Belief
Belief to Faith
Faith to Knowledge
And Knowledge to Embodiment**

This scale is one map: A road to manifestation. Any concept you perceive can elevate from idea to the experience of embodiment. While in the physical world certain actions may be necessary, in the Magical arts, all is intention, as you very well know.

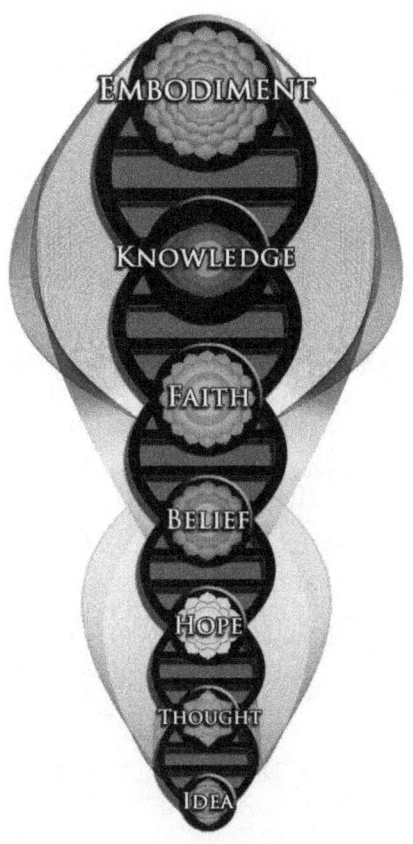

Therefore, for maximum probability of success in any Magical action or plan, consider the state of your intention. Do you believe that your concept is possible? Or do you simply hope it is? How do you shift between the two?

What would be required for you to elevate your belief to a knowing, a certainty of outcome?

You travel this ladder, experiencing every step, slowly or rapidly as fits the situation.

Before moving on, pause and consider one of your life's most important goals. Most goals are held in the mind's eye—for if they were already your experience they would not be on your to-do list.

Practice climbing up this ladder. What mental, emotional, spiritual and physical actions do you feel you must take to elevate the goal to a level of faith; a level of deep convicted knowing of manifestation, before all supporting evidence is physically present?

Pause, and do this now.

MEMORY ASCENSION PRACTICE

Open your mind to the halls of memory. Recall a time where you felt challenged. Possibly depleted, stressed, without the support you desired.

At some point, a choice of how to react had to be made. First mentally, then verbally and physically.

Consider your inner worlds, at that moment. Consider not just what you chose to express, but how you went about making that choice.

Did you fully express your higher self, or did you allow the reactive response of your ego—possibly a response of fear, lack or anger?

Were you aware, in your moment of expression, that other options were available?

Did you choose, in that moment, to see yourself as a Lesser being not possessing of the strength to act as you knew you could act? Perhaps a reason or excuse was made, some justification to keep you where you were at, for that point in the river.

How did this choice affect you, and those around you, spiritually?

What would a higher choice have looked like? A choice aligned more with your highest, truest, best self? Did you really need more resources or support to act in this way? Or was that strength inside of you—and exists there still?

Pause now, and relive the memory. Experience the stimulus, and pause before allowing the response. In the private world of your inner mind, use your imagination to time travel and see the parallel world where you chose differently.

Embody both your past self and your highest self, and choose differently.

Rewrite time.

Rewrite history.

Breathe.

And breathe again.

Are you different? Have you changed?

While higher Magics are required to shift choices to affect the physical world in more dramatic ways—such as regrowing fingers—you might find now that you feel different. You might find that you feel stronger, more empowered, more able and ready to make the choice you wish you made next time a challenging stimulus comes around.

If you have done this faithfully, we offer you a Magical apprenticeship. Your assignment is simple: for thirty days starting now, practice at least 11 minutes of Zen meditation where you notice the pauses between your inhalations and exhalations.

After your meditation, repeat the above exercise. Give yourself ten minutes. Keep a log of your memory before, during and after the shift.

On day 31, record a video log of your progress: How easier it got, how your view of yourself has changed, and how your life as a whole has opened.

If you submit this video to us digitally with permission to share it and inspire other students, you will be engaged in a Karmic partnership where you receive the astral cords of sincere admiration, as your peers see you as strong, as vulnerable, as grown.

If you choose to keep this video to yourself, we offer to you to watch it at least once per month, to remind yourself, to anchor yourself, in your freedom of choice.

Do or do not, and be at peace. We love you, *all* parts of you, unconditionally.

A disclaimer for Memory Magic. The above exercise is an introductory practice. As you ascend and rise in interdimensional capability, you may notice changes in your physical world—including the memories of other beings—with practices like this one.

Expect not, yet be prepared: Of the infinite timelines, infinite versions of your friends and acquaintances, all possibilities exist. As you learn, integrate and apply all teachings of the Magic is Real series, you will have increased capacity for creating change.

Allow whatever is, to be. Force not. Accept. Surrender, and realize that Truth is a relative thing. While your practices to elevate yourself may enable you to see yourself as you wish to be seen, other beings may still see you as you "were."

Whether you choose to edit your memories or practice Memory Ascension simply to remind yourself of your freedom to choose, know that your guides may allow others to see and express different memories of your Lower Self so as to test your patience and compassion.

And legally, of course, always examine evidence. You could make a mental shift without making a physical one, and any statements you make should always coincide with Consensus Physical Reality in a formal setting, regardless of your memories of simultaneous, past or alternate selves, and your Truth as a soul in every Now.

CHOOSING FUTURE TIMELINES

Many situations in life are similar, energetically and psychologically. For the events likely to happen throughout the next week, consider *how* you choose to respond.

Reversing the above exercise, what would a lower choice look like? A choice farther from mastery, closer to immaturity and reactivity?

Take a moment and write out a narrative: The next time challenging situations arises, how can you respond more in line with your highest self? Write at least 3 sentences describing each of: The situation, your inner environment, three ways of responding (normal, higher and lower), and the likely outcomes of each response.

This exercise will help you be more conscious of the reality you create. It is a foundational practice, a way to be Actively Mindful. If you would like another mini-apprenticeship, perform this exercise daily for thirty days, and create a video in the same instance as above.

In our modern era, devoting oneself full time to a live-in situation with a master is impractical for most of us. Digital Apprenticeships (DAs) are great ways to provide an opportunity for a student-teacher relationship at your convenience, and maintain accountability, a balanced exchange of value, and guided training.

These apprenticeships, both overtly mentioned (as above) and subtly provided (as alluded to without as many pointers) are also significantly shorter in duration. Just like taking online courses instead of pursuing a university degree, DAs can help you build experience and credentials.

More interaction is, of course, provided with masterminds and workshops. A variety of options exist to meet you where you are at. Traditional in-person apprenticeships are considered on a case by case basis, last 6 months, and occur in the San Francisco Bay Area for students over 21 years of chronological age.

PARALLEL SELVES

You are awareness.

You have minds and bodies, of infinite variety. The multiverse is vast.

Many of these minds and bodies resemble the one you currently inhabit. Many appear as beings of other gender, height and weight, in different eras with different missions.

As you integrate, your awareness will expand. Just as one hand can pat your head while the other rubs your stomach, you as primary awareness can choose to practice the skill of seeing other versions of you as appendages of embodiment.

The simultaneous awareness of multiple lifetimes will help you shift more quickly next time you wish to work a spell. Whether you call it timeline shifting, dimension hopping, probability altering or reality creation, the ultimate product of your manifestation is what is aligned, experienced and embodied by your awareness in its primary, consistent, consensus reality.

If Magic were simple, everyone would do it.

At the highest levels, you are everyone.

So make it simple! And give yourself time.

Consider what you *know* how you wish to be. Thought, word, deed.

YOU ARE AWARENESS

You are of, and are completely, the infinite body of God. Universe, fully realized Christ, Flying Spaghetti Monster, Source—use the words you love most, and dissolve attachments to things needing to be a certain way.

The All is in All!

Allow yourself, the re-awakening Buddha, to be that which feels most right, most authentic and true, in this moment.

I see you.

I accept you.

I love you, just as you are.

We. Are. One.

9
I Am Awareness

"We read for inspiration. We practice for progress."
-Sifu Brown

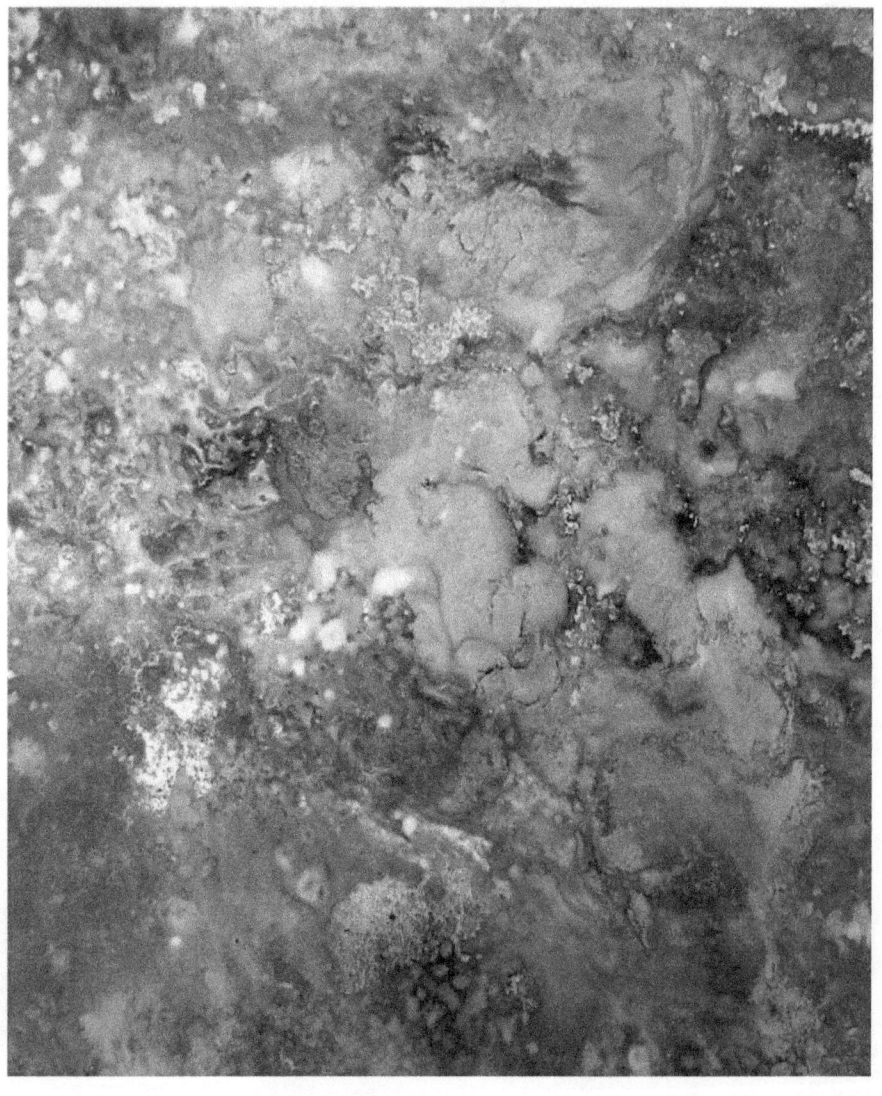

*F*or your progress along the continuum of Enlightenment. For your consistent and escalating manifestations of Miracles. For your permission to **MAKE SPIRITUALITY FUN AGAIN**, and for your Magical and Spiritual Ascension.

Read these and reap 10% of the benefit.

Perform these, and receive 70%.

Embody these with absolute focus and devotion, your best efforts, your highest level performance: gain all you can gain.

This, like life, is a pop quiz. You are fully prepared. This moment will never come again, though your future selves can retake future quizzes and combine their scores.

This is an offering, at a precise time in precise circumstances. Unless the consequences would be dire, proceed immediately, until completion, without pause.

And just now, in your moment of decision, did you practice action, or practice procrastination?

INSTRUCTION:

Repeat aloud with a clear and strong voice. Have conviction.

Visualize as richly and completely as you can.

Focus upward, on the space in the center of your head. The Sanctum Sanctorum; holy of holies; innermost chamber; your Chamber of Secrets.

The eye of Horus.

This is a call and response exercise. The first time you read a statement, encounter it, receive it. The second time, say it aloud.

(read:)
I repeat these words
(speak:)
"I repeat these words"

To Begin Editing my Source Code
"To Begin Editing my Source Code"

I receive this template as an offering
"I receive this template as an offering"

To my Higher Self
"To my Higher Self"

That I May Grow.
"That I May Grow."

May my sixth chakra blossom
"May my sixth chakra blossom"

May it open, detoxify, heal.
"May it open, detoxify, heal."

May it shine brightly with the purple light of awareness
"May it shine brightly with the purple light of awareness"

And may the physical bridge, that is my pineal gland
"And may the physical bridge, that is my Pineal Gland"

Be Perfectly Open, that my Third Eye may See
"Be Perfectly Open, that my Third Eye may See"

I now receive these words
"I now receive these words"

As if they were my own
"As if they were my own"

And for the incantations that follow
"And for the incantations that follow"

May I know them as written by me.
"May I know them as written by me."

And accept them as my own, a message from myself to myself
"And accept them as my own, a message from myself to myself"

"I see the energies of my brain. I see swirling colors around a pink and tan organ, the biological conduit for my consciousness.

"*I am awareness*. I am that which perceives, knowing the object I witness—my current body—as part of me, but not all of me.

"I remember emotion. I remember happiness, and see the event in my life where I can feel it, in my body.

"I see that area of my brain illuminate, a yellow glow.

"I open and feel the serotonin, the dopamine and oxytocin. I smile, call forth the memory, allow it to surface. No thoughts; only experience. I feel the yellow, the event, the chemistry. I know myself in this moment to be happy.

"And I release it, as breath and as color."

"As the color flows, the emotion goes. There is stillness inside me. I am still."

(Breathe four times. Each breath increasing density, brightness, the color and the light. Shine. Power. Your essence. You, the eternal light.)

"I am stillness.

"I am still."

(Pause to reflect, or to continue releasing the emotional charge as color until there is no emotion left.)

"The oneness of universal sound, the eternal Om. Pronounced as Aum, adapted to some cultures as Amen. This word I reclaim in my own Magic, in my own name.

"So I say, long, loud and sincere. Auuuuummmmmmmmm.

"So mote it be."

"I hereby reclaim and restore the traditions of spirituality and religion, and reboot them for our current Age, for Aquarius.

"In this word, my soul and emotion are one, through my body which vocalizes slowly, deeply, richly. Auuuuummm. Aaauuuummmm. Auummmmm.

This book I write for myself; I am the author; I am the word.

The flow of essence sees that which exists as an infinite spectrum of identities and meanings. Of the cycle of life and death as represented in the energies of the goddess, I reclaim my essence as the divine feminine. May she awaken within me, and may every woman I witness—and every man too, feel the balance of the yin and the yang, moon and sun, earth and sky.

I remember the masculine energies, the creative forces of Shiva. Generative, directive. I see the power of these energies embodied in fluids, natural components of reality, representing the spark of life. Having, as above, only the meaning I choose to acknowledge.

I remember gender. I remember its purpose, and the genderless nature of soul. I release the need for labels and language.

I release myself from bondage.

I see myself as an infinite being. May my appearance, in cloth and words and expressions, express the fullness of my soul, as defined by me, fully accepting myself and fully receiving all the acceptance I will ever need.

I am whole.

I step into my truth as a full and complete being. I accept the dualistic illusion of gender in word and in form as part of my school in this world, in this time.

In this, I know the concept of *meaning*, and I know it to be a fabrication.

May all that has meaning be conscious to me. May I be aware of the meanings I hold, and feel permissioned to reprogram these meanings, infinitely, rewriting my own source code, in this body. Through this mind. As this soul.

(Pause for 3 deep, restorative breaths.)

I am of the collective known as God, expressed as the awareness I am.

I am all thoughts that arise, and none of them. I am he who refuses the call, and he who answers. I am she who knows herself as all things and no things. I am awareness.

I am that.

I recognize myself as living in greater clarity, in every day, in every way. I feel my knowing residing within me, beyond the need for interpretation, beyond the need for thought. I know the truth of my intuition, that spark of omniscience—divine self-realization in the container that is my life.

I recognize this life as one of my many lives, in all times, places, and parallel worlds. My consciousness encompass all, and may my mind receive what it needs, in every moment of now.

I say these words, and return to life, as it was. No more, no less but a moment of vibration, if only in the secret of my inner deepest thoughts.

May my thoughts be honored. May they be seen and felt as safe. May my thoughts represent my intentions, and may they be chosen consciously. May all of my thoughts be aligned with my highest and truest self, in clarity, at all times good.

I will be free of suffering. My thoughts will support this.

I wish for all beings to be free of suffering. My thoughts support this.

I am that I am. And I am enough.

I live freely, feeling as I choose to feel. I am hereby liberated from condition-response, from the stimuli that evoked reaction in a former mind and body. I am the light of consciousness that moves between worlds, and I choose the enlightenment that is right for me in this moment, in all moments henceforth.

So mote it be.

(Aum, deeply and richly, seven times. During each Aum, feel, see and know the reality, in your minds eye. Experience that which you have just called forth, and see yourself feeling, acting, living the incantations you have just evoked.

You are a powerful wizard. And that was one beautiful spell.)

10
How to Feel Your Chi

"I am not the body. I am the light coming out of it."
-Michael Monk

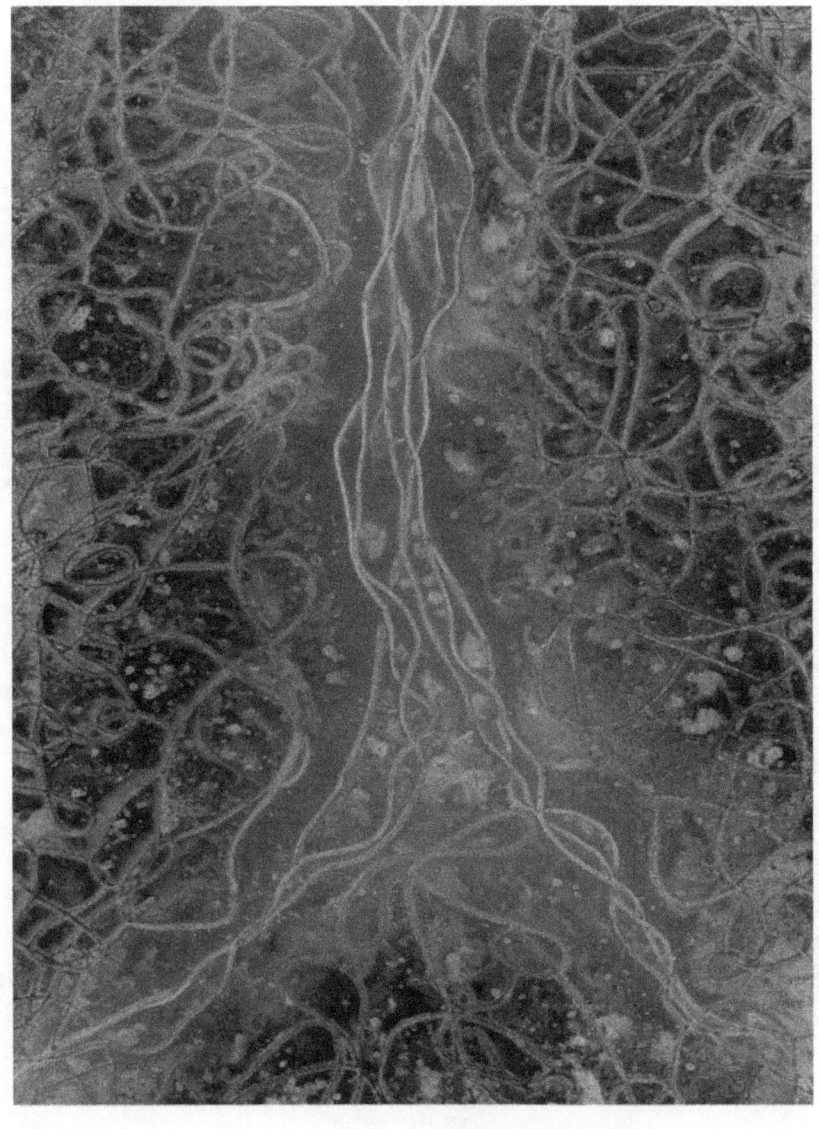

The vital life force energy of the body goes by many names: Qi / Chi (Chinese), Ki (Japanese), Prana (Hindi and Damanhurian) and Biofield Energy in the West. We mix up the words to get you comfortable and familiar with their interchangeability.

Feeling Prana is critical if you want to work the subtler levels of the field that include the bioenergetic, ethereal and electromagnetic. It's a great place to start, since there's so many resources for you to learn, and Chi has been researched and documented for thousands of years.

Many good energy healing programs like the Barbara Brennan School of Healing will help you build these fundamental skills in a guided environment, with experienced practitioners, and a large group of fellow students. It's best if you follow specific exercises that have been tested, refined, and shown successful to help new students build their vital life force energy, and awaken enhanced physical, mental, and spiritual abilities.

When I first learned Reiki, it was in a casual setting as part of a 25-minute discussion and a quick, informal initiation. I learned about a symbol and demonstrated two basic techniques for several seconds, got feedback, and was told "okay, now you can go practice!"

An ego solely identified with the mind would call that bad teaching. As I later learned, **life is the best teacher**, and my instinct, intuition, and guides led to an improvement of technique to the point that now, almost every cooperative person I work with can feel my Prana - often significantly.

But I'm a rare breed, and most of my Pranic developed later in life, once I received significant instruction. While it's true real world experience can be a great teacher, having maps of the physical and energetic bodies, learning how your astral form is affected by your emotions, drugs and diet—and charging or clearing an environment energetically are hugely valuable skills that benefit greatly from good explanations.

MAGICAL SCIENCE

How do energy workers measure their skills, their strength, their effectiveness? Are the popular books we know of today the industry's best, or simply the ones that have survived persecution?

It's not unheard of that some pharma companies, with their multi-billion-dollar advertising budgets, would engage in efforts, both direct and subtle, to discredit energy healing and energy work. If you dig deeply enough (or perhaps if you dig at all), you'll find a field littered with skeptics—individuals not so thoroughly educated as to have an informed an opinion, yet vehemently saying "that isn't real!" or "there's no proof!" and finding any angle they can to discredit legitimate evidence.

Ridicule is probably one of the most hurtful things to the ego of a new student. Even though we're working on transmuting emotions and refining our egos to merge them with our souls—even with all the stuff about detachment and Be The Witness, we're talking about societal impressions here, and the disservice to an Art when it is passed down with poor and incomplete teaching.

Only with more schools, more transparency in the teachings, more certifications and more scientific data can we truly qualify and quantify the difference between a healer (or a psychic) and a fraud. There is a way to fix this, if we choose to recognize it. Ladies and gentlemen and everyone else, I hereby proclaim:

The era of Magical Science has begun!

There's a chicken and an egg scenario when people can go around and say "I do Reiki" yet can't represent the level of their skill—or worse, their effectiveness. If you want a dentist, Yelp and other sites can give you ratings and reviews. Research physicians can tell you the percentage of patients who are successfully affected by a treatment. We need more people and more tools to help us do the same with energetic healing.

We need to draw back the Bamboo Curtain and really take an uncensored look at the 5000+ year old history of medical Qigong in China.

We need to be real with ourselves about the truth of the origin of the human race, examine the archaeological evidence and historical records about the beings with large bodies and long heads that were prevalent in Egypt and Sumeria, and consider the Magicians and Healers of those eras, and consider where they received their information, advanced as it was for that age.

We need to remember how knowledge becomes discovered and lost. We need to stop and realize that most people have heard of *Atlantis*, and many disagree of what, when, and where it was. We need to remember that even in the United States, with all its innovations and marketing, the standard procedures for nutrition, fitness and even child raising can change drastically decade to decade.

How surprising then would it be to realize that this science has been performed before, the discoveries made and the research found—only to simply fall out of fashion?

Or be suppressed. Repressed. Hidden.

The term "Occult" derives from "Occluded," meaning "Hidden." There's nothing mysterious, dark or woo-woo about it. With all the information in the world and all the interesting parties wanting to take credit to further their careers, it's no surprise that methods of healing traditionally passed down between compassionate, selfless individuals...gets buried.

So where do we start? Start actually learning the truth about Chi, and being convinced that it is real?

Start separating fact from fiction?

Start realizing some things that sound like fiction—such as masters standing with all their weight on one finger, painting while standing on eggshells, and stopping bullets with their bare palms—these things are actually possible with dedicated training, just like any other complex skill?

Complicating the matter is the large volume of information available. A read through Barbara Brennan's *Hands of Light* or *Core Light Healing* can give you some mental proficiency of her system. You'll also learn fundamental truths that translate into other modalities. But comparing the Brennan method to your local acupuncturist's hands on Qigong therapy? Good luck!

Only with a larger and more mature industry can we truly rate, compare and improve, innovating on the ancient sciences just like western medicine has helped advance the knowledge of acupuncture by showing—with fMRIs—more of what's occurring during a treatment.

A WORLD OF SUPPORTERS

While it's true more and more devices are spreading that can sense the subtle energies involved in hands-on and psychic healing, a quick Google search shows (as of this writing) no leading company, no widely acclaimed household product sold next to Band-Aids and hydrogen peroxide... at least not in the west!

I hope that will change. Will you be the one to help change it?

I know I will. A significant portion of all Magic is Real proceeds will be devoted to Magical research—deepening our understanding of the sciences currently out of the grasp of the general public, exploring the boundaries of what's possible with Pranic Healing and extending those boundaries with groundbreaking experiments that involve hundreds of healers, crystal and sacred geometry arrays, and powerful, clear intentions.

And to be honest, most practitioners that I've met, as skilled as they were, only knew about how their patients responded.

Psychologists would call this the difference between procedural and declarative memory; Howard Gardner would compare Linguistic and Bodily-kinesthetic Intelligence. Let's add

Energetic intelligence to the mix; those who do *can* teach, if they so choose to develop the skill. One of the highly skilled practitioners I respect is Anna-Lisa Adelberg, a devoted, loving woman who teaches in the bay area of California, along with Raina DeLear and a fantastic team of assistant teachers and staff. Her school, Luminous Awareness Institute, can be found at luminousawareness.com.

Thinking as a scientist, when you look up research supporting the existence of the human energy field, you find organizations abound like William Tiller institute at http://www.tillerinstitute.com, and Chi.is. When you research Remote Viewing, you find tons of talks and downloadable instruction, and even when you look up the measurement of consciousness, you see organizations like the International Remote Viewing Association.

For years, the app SyncTXT generated synchronicities by picking up on elements of your field *through your phone* and having an AI sort through a bank of meaningful quotes, sending you the right ones at the right time.

Sadly, as the control for information heats up, the pressure to discredit legitimate organizations that study psychic phenomena rises as well. Now, as often happens as the slow-to-evolve mainstream uses PR campaigns to discredit things that don't fit in the model, the first results that can be found of Princeton's PEAR lab are discrediting statements. Their data of psychic phenomena still exists to show, as their site used to say, "tangible, measurable information independent of distance or time (that) challenges the foundation of any reductionist brain-based model of consciousness."

Look deeply enough, in one corner of the web or another, and you just might find it, and other sources. As is safe for us, we will compile such data and make it available to you.

When I was editing the chapter, *Wind and Rain*, the message "The most profound statements are often said in silence" arrived *exactly* as I was finishing the part about invisible discussions with your spirit guide.

Talk about woo-woo... Married with tech!

The founder of this app, Adam Curry, is a good friend with a history of pioneering research into technology that can interface with consciousness. He's also a founder of *Entangled* (consciousness-app.com), "A radical new technology to explore the power of consciousness and the nature of reality. The world's largest consciousness research project in a free app." We've had the most trippy chats about Joe Rogan and the Annunaki...

Speaking of aliens, an Alpha Centaurian was rumored to be the teacher of William Bengston, author of *The Energy Cure*, researcher at Indiana and Brown university (among others), and Man Who Has Been Documented To Repeatedly Heal Mice Of Lethal Stages of Cancer.

When I studied with Bill, I learned that he was also president of the Society for Scientific Exploration, which focuses on "Peer-reviewed research on consciousness, physics, alternative energy, healing, and more."

If you want to be part of this incredible Magical scientific revolution and help organize the info on applied consciousness in an incredible wiki, please reach out.

CHI AND PSYCHIC ABILITIES

Working with Prana is working on the subtle body, the part of you that is generally invisible to the physical eye, yet visible to the inner senses, has distinct levels of vitality, intensity and function. Barbara Brennan, who was a NASA Physicist before becoming a spiritual healer, describes Heightened Sense Perception (HSP), and states on her school's Facebook page:

> *"The reality is that HSP is normal for all human beings. It has been used in different cultures for many millennia, in religion and in healing work. Many native people still rely on it for gathering information about those who are ill and how to heal them.*

> *When Christianity and then the scientific revolution swept Europe, the Church forbade the use of HSP, associating it with darkness, paganism and the devil. As science came to power, it increasingly regarded HSP as superstition and fantasy. Under that kind of pressure, it rapidly fell out of use.*
>
> *Now, in the new millennium, the importance of high sense perception is being rediscovered."*

Along with the Institute of Noetic Sciences and many other notable organizations, Brennan is one of the leaders in in the field. In 2011, she was listed by the Watkins Review as the 94th most spiritually influential person in the world.

Perhaps you've already felt Chi in your own body—as tingling, heat, cold, electricity or magnetism. These are in actuality different types of energy, just like there are different types of specialized brain cells.

Just as anyone with fully functional eyes can learn to see 50 shades of gray, so too can anyone with a functioning Sixth Chakra (Pineal gland, Eye of Horus) learn to see and feel Prana.

If you or someone you know can't feel Prana right away—whether alone or with a skilled practitioner—take heart, and be patient. We're talking about *subtle*. Your perceptions grow with use, just like your ability to stand on one leg.

As your nervous system develops with practice, and the dendritic connections of your brain grow, you will develop this inner sense and it will strengthen over time.

'Show' is, in this case, superior to 'Tell'. You can tell anyone all the information you like about Prana and energy medicine, but showing them in their own bodies will achieve a quicker and stronger realization for most people. Let's start by testing your perception.

EXERCISE: BUILD A PRANIC SUN

Step 1:

Sit up or stand up (whatever feels more energizing), spine straight.

Step 2:

Breathe fully and deeply three times until you are centered, aligned and calm. Relax your belly and your face, and if you feel tension elsewhere in your body, offer it a few loud sighs to release. For the inner senses to be clear—especially for a beginner—it's best if the outer senses are calm. Not too hungry, full, cold or warm; aim for stillness and alignment. If you need to become calm, meditate with deep, rich breathing.

Step 3:

Hold your hands out in front of you, about six inches apart and facing each other. Focus with a relaxed gaze on the space between them. For stronger sensation, practice with a friend facing you, mirroring your motions and breath.

As Dr. Strange taught us, fully intact bodies aren't necessary for Magic. All beings have access to Prana, and if you only have one hand, you can visualize the other, or modify as needed. If your body is otherwise altered from the norm, modify this and any other exercise as feel intuitively best.

Step 4:

As you inhale, pull your hands apart another six inches, so they're about twelve inches apart. As you exhale, push your hands together.

Step 5:

Inhale again, pulling your hands apart. Visualize streams of golden light flowing with your breath, going into your chest, your back, your heart. Exhale, and as you move your hands closer together, see the energy flowing down into your arms. It passes your shoulders, your elbows, forearms, your wrists, and exits through your hands, from a golden sun in the center of your palms.

Step 6:

Inhale, pull your hands apart. Call forth more golden rays of energy. Relax your upper body, feel it flowing into you.

Repeat this 7 more times. See a sparkling golden sun growing between your hands. As your palms come together, imaging you're squishing it like a large, Magical sponge. Try to feel the pressure.

After the warmup, exhale completely, and allow your hands to come closer together to about 6 inches apart. Begin to slowly push them closer until the distance decreases to about two inches. As you exhale, feel more energy coming from of your palms. As you inhale, pull your hands apart again, but maintain the 2-6 inch "Squished Sun Sponge" space of greater density.

Repeat this process until you feel your Chi, or for up to twenty breaths. You may begin to feel a pressure between your hands. You may feel tingling, warmth, or a magnetic pulse. If not, take heart; just like learning to play music, the ability and strengthening of your nervous system comes with time.

About 90% of my private students can feel their Chi. If you haven't ever worked with energy before and are doing this alone, you may need to give it 4-5 sessions. Allow one sleep cycle to pass between each; just like when you first learned how to read, feeling and working with Chi is using your brain in a new way. The information exists in an organized fashion, and bit by bit, you can and will master it in accordance with your effort and dedication.

If inspired, play with distances, breath and visualizations until you customize the method to serve you best. Feel your Prana. Enjoy it!

Once you can feel your own chi, experiment with trees, crystals and other people. See if you can sense them, tuning into them with the unique perception you're developing.

As the chi ball between your hands grows, you can also experiment with moving it around your body. Directing chi towards your third eye, for example, will help open and strengthen it; this is true for all chakras.

Remember to stay grounded, and for every upper chakra you work on, invest an equal amount of time on a lower chakra, until you have an innate understanding of how balanced your system is.

These practices should always be done with proper instruction, since too much energy in one chakra can cause an imbalance. Often those with anxiety or heightened sensitivity have an excess of Prana in the upper chakras and not enough strength in their lower ones. Grounding exercises, and a daily Qigong practice with bare feet in contact with the earth, and a deeper squat to open the root chakra can help with this, along with the proper use of Chinese herbs and Breathing techniques.

This chapter is meant as an introduction. Bruce Frantzis, Lee Holden and Adam Atman have detailed instructions in print and online if you want to go deeper.

Just like if the muscles of one hamstring are tighter than another, you may realize that, as with stretching and strengthening, you can heal and tonify (a Chinese Medicine word for "strengthen energetically") any part of your body.

MEDITATION RESOURCES

Your ability to work with Prana will increase with a dedicated mediation practice. As you focus deeply and for sustained amounts of time, that same muscle can be applied to energy work.

Meditation has shown to increase intelligence, reduce stress and anxiety, and expand consciousness https://www.ncbi.nlm.nih.gov/pubmed/15534199. The time more than pays for itself, as noted in the Harvard Business Review article "*If You're Too Busy To Meditate, Read This.*"

The apps Calm and Headspace offer guided meditations that are excellent for beginners. Wearable technology from Heartmath will help you sync your breathing and heartbeat via portable biofeedback, and the Muse headset from ChooseMuse.com will give you realtime feedback based on your brain waves.

Tools can be very effective tools to help you build a practice. Just as exercise strengthens the body, meditation can heal, strengthen and refine the mind and spirit.

PURIFY AND STRENGTHEN WITH TREE POSE

I recommend the Building a Pranic Sun exercise three times a day for a month. Each practice should take about five minutes, and the Magical Fun of Chi Superpowers should be a great motivation to meditate if you aren't already inspired. The probability of you feeling your Prana and development of basic working skills with it is nearly guaranteed if you follow this practice with devotion, and likely you'll pick it up within several days.

Once you build proficiency in chi, you'll even be able to affect your musculoskeletal systems. Any time I'm feeling sore, tight, toxic, tired, ungrounded, or anything off center, I go outside (or play music inside) and perform a short self-healing practice.

One of the simplest and most powerful methods of building your chi flow is the posture "Tree Pose," or Zhan Zhuang.

In southern China, this is often pronounced as "Jam Jong." Holding Tree Pose will circulate the qi in your body, strengthening it, and often condensing it where your body needs it most. For example, if one leg or arm is inflamed or sore, you might feel muscle tension as you stand still, holding this pose. That tension is often a buildup of chi clearing out toxins and strengthening the tissues as your system's natural intelligence heals itself.

I used to go to a chiropractor and get massage therapy often. Qigong - especially this pose - helped me realize I could simply stand still, apply my willpower, and regain physical balance.

It's portable. It's effective. And it's free!

While as a reminder this isn't medical advice, many of my students and those who train with master Adam Atman (adamatman.com) report a cessation of diseases of all types. Adam has recommended holding Tree Pose for one hour a day for six months to cure chronic ailments. While this may sound like quite a commitment, it's far less of an ordeal than a lifetime of doctor appointments, with the waiting, expenses, side effects, and feeling cruddy at short term solutions which often cover up symptoms rather than healing the root cause.

To practice tree pose, stand with your feet parallel and shoulder width apart. Bend your knees slightly and feel your heels on the ground. Relax your pelvis, and allow the knees to gently shift outwards. Keep your whole foot flat on the floor, and your spine perfectly straight.

As if you were hugging an invisible tree, hold your arms out, elbows bent, and palms facing you. The simplest pose is the one where your arms aren't elevated but parallel with the ground; however, I've found that if you have neck issues, holding your arms higher helps, just as if you have pelvic issues, you can hold your arms lower, palms facing in towards the second chakra, and allow the chi to gather there.

As you allow your shoulders to drop, breathe slowly and deeply. Depending on how much time you can devote to your practices, this pose can double as a concentration exercise. Just as with sitting meditation, sensations in your body may arise to distract you. Similarly, you'll want to be patient with yourself, starting with a manageable amount of time of 10 minutes, and increasing by one minute daily.

If you commit to doing this for even ten minutes, you might notice certain detoxification indicators like releasing of gas from the mouth or rectum, increased flow of mucus, slight increase in heartbeat, and possible racing of thoughts. As you breathe deeply, maintain spinal alignment, and sink into the posture, you'll practice mastery over your body and will allow it to do its work.

Once the detox process is finished (it gets shorter with more consistent practice, and usually doesn't last more than 20 minutes if you maintain an otherwise healthy lifestyle), and sometimes even before then, you'll notice an increase of chi in your body. This might feel like a buzzing vibration, and if you're sensitive, you'll feel the tingles all over your skin.

Just like meditation, decide on the length of time in advance, and don't cheat. This posture may be more physically uncomfortable, but unless you feel like your body is literally becoming injured, stay with it. As with lifting weights, certain sensations may feel uncomfortable but be to your highest benefit. A local instructor, or at least someone to help by phone or video, can help guide you and confirm proper alignment and technique.

In the beginning, do what you need to do in order to focus. Ideally, listen to the sounds of nature or simple music without lyrics you understand. Don't watch anything digitally unless your mind and body are really fighting back; if so it's best to watch something very, very simple, like the visuals of Electric Sheep, so your awareness is free to keep watch over your body. Ideally, build up to eyes closed, like with most meditation practices.

For all dedicated students, this is a required daily practice.

Try it now. Set a timer for 5-10 minutes, and see how you feel. Of all the practices in this book, Tree Pose is one of the most universally beneficial.

PRACTICE MAKES POWERFUL

Everything is connected. If you are good at *feeling* in general, you will have an advantage in being able to feel your Prana.

Classes in Tai Chi, Qigong and Kundalini Yoga can help tremendously, especially if the instructor is live and provides real-time feedback.

If you practice Pranic Sun with a friend, whoever who feels less sensation can place their left between the hands of the person who feels it more strongly. It's fun to experiment building Pranic Suns before and after Tree Pose to really see the difference!

Sharing Magical techniques can be fun. If you have a friend with no experience in chi and you're wondering how likely they are to feel it, your best chances are with someone who is connected to their emotions, who is able to slow down, and who is a good listener. You can say "Hey, want to feel your chi? It'll only take 2 minutes, and can change your life!"

When willing participants succeed, their eyes go wide. "Magic is Real, baby!" And you just did it.

There are many factors that affect your Prana, and your ability to perceive it. Just like your strength, and your analytical and creative abilities can wax and wane, your ability to feel and project Prana may oscillate based on your sleep, diet, stress, environment, toxins, social support, emotions, physical energy, mental energy, and even the moon phases.

You don't have to memorize all this stuff unless you want to walk the path towards mastery. As you approach it, after practicing 10-20 hours a week for years—the above factors will both matter less, and like the highest levels of Magic and manifestation, you will only need your consciousness.

SPIRITUAL ENERGY AND BIOCHEMISTRY

Feeling Prana, and drawing it forth, is one of my favorite Minor Magical Powers. If I'm tired, I can summon forth vast amounts to energize the body. If I'm de-motivated, I can lie down, get very still, and draw forth a type of Qi called Shen to raise my spirits. If I feel inflammation in the body, I can focus and project it outwards as heat. There are some Chinese masters who can even create fire with their Qi, as demonstrated repeatedly on YouTube.

If you practice Prana work regularly, you will slowly and steadily gain the capacity to:

- Draw energy forth from the universe and direct it to strengthen your mind, body and spirit.
- Increase your vital energy—literally that which keeps you awake, alert, and alive.
- Heal more quickly
- Have a stronger intuition
- Project your chi so others can feel it *(this takes considerably more practice—start with supportive close friends, and stay humble.)*

WAYS TO BUILD YOUR PRANA:

- Eat healthy. Organic fruits and vegetables, non-processed foods. Clean protein from the healthiest sources you can find. Spirulina and activated charcoal taken properly can detoxify your system, and as always, professional advice and laboratory testing is key to assess your health.

- A microbiome free of parasites like candida, and rich in prebiotics and probiotic flora will help you absorb nutrients, maintain a stable mood and weight, and maintain healthy hormone levels.

- Minimal or zero amounts of alcohol or mind altering substances. If you have been consuming naturally grown plant medicines, you may wish to consider taking a break until you can share all of your activities with a skilled and experienced mentor, who can help you understand fully, from an energetic and physical perspective, how you are affecting your brain and organs.

Recreational drugs can imbalance your system. Altered states of consciousness from these and other methods can heighten perception and show you a level of advancement far beyond your current level—however, for their side effects, and the possibility of habituation, I recommend pausing their use until you fully understand what they do to your body, how to mitigate side effects, and considering if you really need them, or are self-medicating for something which can be healed rather than avoided.

Intelligently designed, carefully planned, measured, researched, customized, well advised and intentional purposes are key.

Because these substances can alter your perception, you will need to replicate and verify everything you experience in an altered state while "clean" and validate what appears to be knowledge and very well may be, yet also may not.

Significant research is being performed on psilocybin, ayahuasca, MDMA, and cannabinoids for healing and consciousness expanding purposes. Just as you wouldn't practice a backflip over concrete without supervision and training (and even then, the mats are probably better), so too should you not mistake general information for that which applies to your specific scenario.

Given the growing use of plant medicines, some additional info: They generally deplete your chi (as a word for physical vitality, rather than the general term) and transmute it into Shen (Spiritual energy).

If you have decided independently to use them, you may be curious about the habits of practicing Shamans and Alchemists who partake 1-2 times per month for specific purposes. Daily and even weekly use can cause an imbalance in the system that, depending on the amount and your sensitivity, can take a lot of work to repair.

While use of plant medicines has also been reported to help awaken clairvoyant abilities, they can also let in darker spirits. Compulsions or justifications of anger, sexual inappropriateness, impaired judgment, rash decision making, and heightened fear are some of the potential side effects of using medicines without the ideal set and setting, or with overuse.

The highs and huge boosts to creativity also reflect a neurological shift. As more blood goes to the right side of the brain, and to the temporal prefrontal gyrus which is responsible for intuition, less blood can flow to the Dorsolateral Prefrontal Cortex, the seat of our "Executive Functions" of logical thinking, planning and decision making. The word "Integration" refers to both coming "back to the real world" and giving yourself time to rebalance neurologically.

Just like when drunk, your capabilities change, the same can happen with plant medicine use. For these reasons, along with an unintentional deadly overdose of one of my dear friends, I've begun an intensive research project to provide resources and instruction to help you get in altered states of consciousness without taking medicines or drugs.

I've also started opening people's third eyes energetically through the laying on of hands. Offering transmissions can be a fast and clean way to level up, but of course it's limited to those I can meet with in person.

- Dragon Herbs is a fantastic organization to call [ask for an Herbalist] for recommendations on building your spiritual energy (Shen) naturally. As your Shen rises, your access to channeling, creativity, energy work and similar abilities will also rise.

- Men, you can strengthen your reserves of Qi by refraining from ejaculation, or at least cutting down frequency. This may take some getting used to, and it's absolutely worthwhile. There are advanced tantric techniques to ejaculate while not losing energy, but the simplest way around this is to enjoy sexual activity, stop before you feel like you're even approaching even the urge, and mindfully yet gently pull the energy back into you. A book full of techniques and in depth instruction is *The Multi-Orgasmic Man* by Mantak Chia, who also wrote *The Multi-Orgasmic Woman*.

- Introductory Tantra (working with the sexual energies of the body) and can be performed by all genders to build up sexual energy, then shifting it to a location where you feel depleted.

Many pro athletes do this before a competition. Again, be advised of balance. While finding a live instructor is ideal, this practice isn't yet common in the west. I recommend at last five hours of research before trying these techniques, and at that point, start small, in five minute increments.

Solitary practice is preferable unless you have a very mindful and loving partner and you are both aligned. Neediness and the psychology behind sex with others can interfere with spiritual growth work in a major way, which is why traditionally many monks have been celibate. I'm not suggesting that could be right for your system.

Practicing Tantra with a fully aware, present, mature and energy conscious partner is completely different from the superficial, orgasm-centric sexual activities that seem so common. Quitting porn can help with many things, including this area of your life. The rapid-fire images and stimulation can result in addictions and tendencies that aren't in harmony with our normal mental and biological rhythms, and create objectification and emotional detachment, along with an unnatural hunger, that will lead you to depleting your energy in ways which won't serve your Magical and energetic development.

Most importantly when considering any teacher is finding someone with the utmost respect and consideration. You should never feel forced, compelled or persuaded to do anything in any way, and techniques can be discussed while fully clothed. If something feels wholesome, grounded and true to you, great. If not, trust your intuition and stay safe.

It should go without saying that mixing sex and drugs can amplify the effects of each, both desirable and undesirable. Mindfulness is key. There are so many ways to enhance your consciousness naturally.

Don't get caught up in the trap of justifying pleasure by calling it "spiritual" when you know deep down that if you shared all the details of your intentions and activities with a respected teacher, they wouldn't agree.

Of course, this isn't a blanket prohibition, and amplified states can take you places you couldn't go to normally. Just consider the benefits, risks and alternatives. Consider the next 10 years of your life, and practices that you can do sustainably, consistently, while traveling, and in groups.

Since group fields, daily practices, and deep focus all amplify Magical power, I recommend breathwork as the overall best way to enhance consciousness.

Get updates via MagicalGoldenAge.com and in future books for detailed instructions on natural ways to achieve altered and enhanced states of consciousness, such as holotropic breathing, pranayama (yogic breath control exercises), use of lights, magnets and binaural beats, fasting, Kundalini practices, and other techniques

- In Damanhurian Alchemy School, we learned to record precise details for any type of experiment; the same would benefit you, as your own personal scientist, so you can measure and replicate good results, and avoid poor ones. Your activities, food and liquid intake, exercise, environment, state of mind, peers, intentions and results all matter when considering which actions to take now and in the future Whatever your choices, be safe!

Of course, it needs to be said for liability that I and we don't endorse any use of drugs or illegal activity.

You can also build healthy Pranic levels by getting sufficient sleep, feeling and savoring positive emotion, avoiding EMF pollution and avoiding toxic individuals, since you won't have to use your energy to protect yourself.

Regular practice of Tai Chi, Qigong and any other physical exercise done mindfully and energetically is a great daily habit as well. You can even turn running and weight training into a personalized Qigong with mindfulness and breath, once you have good focus and visualization. If building Prana, Qi or Shen is a priority for you, consider the arts that have been honed for thousands of years before reinventing the wheel.

- Prana is a major component of Magical Strength. Larger Workings require larger amounts of energy, and high daily energy levels can help you make Magic commonplace. The more serious you take your training, the faster you'll progress.

- As your practice grows, so too will your health improve, and your need for sleep may gradually decrease. The time will pay for itself in many ways.

May the force be with you!

11
A Miraculous Healing

"The healer must be well grounded and able to be present and clear in all four dimensions of being at once: the physical, human energy field, hara, and core essence dimensions."

-Barbara Brennan

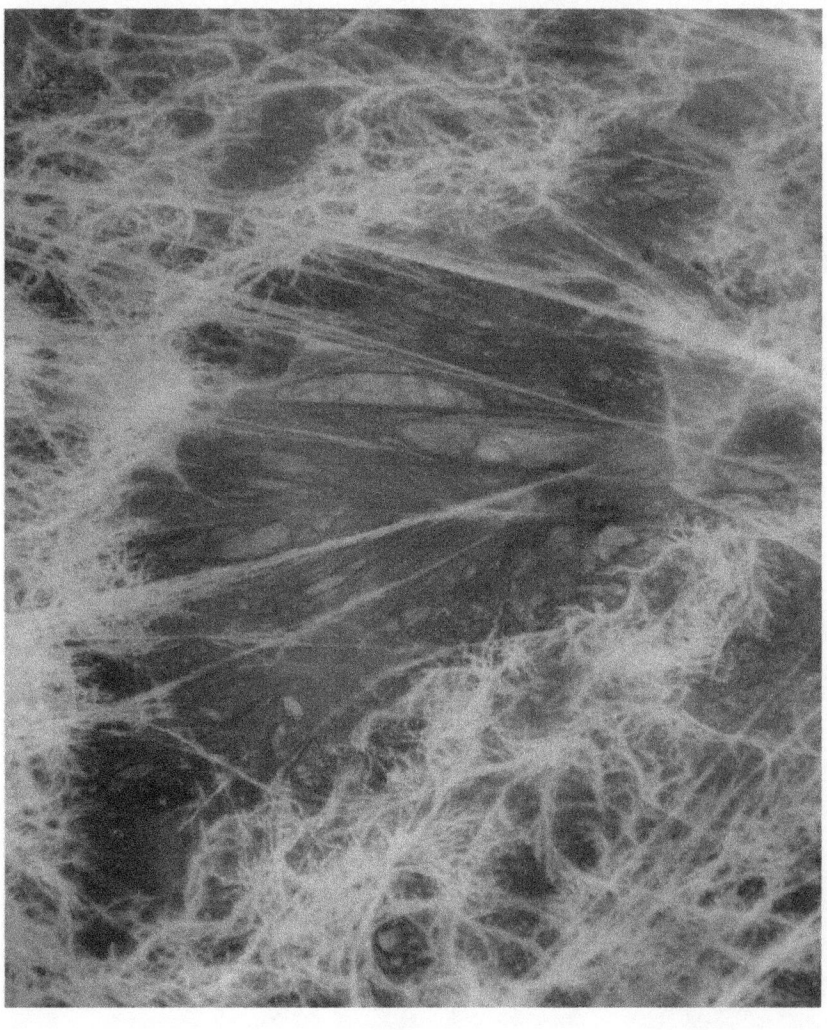

This is one of the most important Magical events of my life.

In the summer of 2007, I was 22 and had achieved the biggest business victory in my then 4-year career as an entrepreneur. I ran a home improvement marketing company, a simple and perfect industry as it allowed me to work with simple products and services and learn the fundamentals of supporting myself outside of the constraints of being an employee.

This built foundational skills that could transfer to almost any field, and allowed me to make my own schedule and be free.

My goal that summer was to achieve $100,000 in contracts. I knew that if I could do that as a student working part time, then I could definitely run a company big enough to provide a good living after school. Later on, after business expenses, I ended up earning $94,000 my first year after graduation due to this business, which was seasonal and only needed attention eight months per year.

I reached my $100k sales goal on June 24th. I still remember the feeling in my car, looking at my clipboard and the signed check of a deposit, catapulting me over my goal early. Elated, I was on top of the world. So thrilled, in fact, that I wondered what greater goals merited attention— and ended up securing $256k that year.

This was a time when my focus was almost entirely material. Save for a casual meditation practice and intellectual engagement with Taoist philosophy, I wasn't studying Magic, much less working it consciously. I wasn't praying, I wasn't chanting mantras. I wasn't even curious. Yet life has a way of waking us up, of reminding us why we're here, no matter how far distracted we may have become.

A celebratory dinner with my two top managers was designed to reflect on the past, and plan for the future. We met at Blue Nile Ethiopian restaurant in Ann Arbor, MI.

By then, in August, right before school started, I didn't walk into dinner excited, positive or happy. It felt like an obligation. I was reminded of my initial goal in launching a business: to learn how to build a successful company so my artwork could thrive, my creative dream of being a professional artist like Dali or Chihuly could be realized, and because I wanted to build a life as an artist, not for something that was just a means to an end.

(I now know that Service and Surrender can lead to ultimate fulfillment... if only Michael A. Singer's extraordinary books were on the reading list... years of strive would have never been. But then, the ego's wounds of looking back at those years wouldn't have existed as things to be healed, and the gifts that arose from them wouldn't exist either. As I look back now, I align with gratitude.)

At that time, most nagging was this distracting voice in my head that said "You're farther away from your chosen path." There was this knowing, deep down, that even art, with its joyful delights and brilliantly vibrant colors wasn't my primary path in this life. It was fun, thrilling, beautiful, a way to connect and share with others... but it wasn't "it."

I sat there, with my managers Mike and Steve, wondering how long I had to keep up the front of politeness, the front of caring about drywall and painting and power washing. Wondering if they noticed my lack of sincerity, despite what I felt were pretty decent acting skills and a practiced front of enthusiasm.

Lying to myself, lying to them, about how interested I was...hurt. The liberating powers of true authenticity weren't fully known to me until later in life, resulting in the book you are now reading.

Suddenly that which should have saved me filled me with dread. I felt a cold chill up my spine, noticed the goosebumps, the raising of hairs. A sense that something really, really bad was about to happen...had already happened...took over my mind with no rational explanation. I saw my dad was calling—dad never called—and I stepped away to take it.

"I saw the doctor last week for a routine colonoscopy," he said, in a regular, level voice, "and the test results came back."

And I knew why he was calling me and there would be no other reason that he was going to say, "I have cancer."

Those were his words, coming from a man who had never been sick for more than a few days, who worked hard and worked out, who had social support and enjoyed casual poker games in the nicer parts of Detroit, who I used to play Squash with and who was the emblem of stability, the emblem of strength.

And as all that raced out of my head in less than a second, I automatically thought, "Ohh, fuck fuck fuck" for about a second—and then I realized I had to be the supportive son, not freak out, appear grounded, give him what *he needed.* I would want the same for myself.

So I said, "Wow. What can they do about it? What are you planning on doing? How are you feeling? What can I do to help?"

My dad, bless his soul as a compassionate and kind man, did a big thing for me—in saying he wanted me to focus on school and work, those things that were important, and that he would deal with this himself.

He cared about self-reliance, and while in the present day I might have the ability and patience and tenderness and kindness and love in my heart to help him, back then... I didn't. Growing up in a male-dominated, heteronormative, suburban society, I barely recognized half of my emotions, much less knew how to process them.

My mind became coldly practical, in the days that followed.

It was 2007, Michigan was going into a recession before the rest of the country. I interviewed for and received the beginnings of an offer from Google, but really wanted my own business, for the freedom and lack of income ceiling that provided. Now, with a sick parent, the final straw: There was *no way* I could accept a new job and have to jump on a call, or drive 60 minutes to an ER on short notice. I needed the freedom only entrepreneurship could provide.

Fast forward through the months of doctor consultations, chemotherapy, and endless hours of waiting. I'm on my way to Whole Foods, and got a call that dad was rushed to the ER.

The nurse said that his intestines had literally *burst* during a colonoscopy. The inflammation of his guts from months of chemo may have played a factor, and he was being prepped for emergency surgery. He could die at any moment.

Random facts from biology came into mind. If the colon bursts, that means all of the stuff inside—stuff your body is purposefully keeping from the rest of itself—is getting everywhere. Polluting healthy tissue. Creating acidic burns. This was a pretty shitty scenario.

Time blurs. I arrive at the hospital, wait with mom, and we hear that dad really wasn't doing well. Mom and I are talking in the waiting room, an elevator opens and the kidney doctor comes out in scrubs that don't look entirely clean.

He had a somber look on his face and a hand twice its usual gripping strength is connected to a voice "Oh God, oh God, please let him be okay," and I just knew that something was up because doctors don't just leave in the middle of a surgery unless the best or the worst has already happened and was this it, this was too soon he was so young and wait let the doctor speak.

"Would you like to talk in a private room?" Mom can't get up. We ignore the others nearby while they did their best to pretend they weren't listening. We encouraged the doctor to speak.

"Larry's kidneys aren't functioning," he said. I'm going to try and get them going and try to help them work, but ultimately he's going to need dialysis—for this level of shutdown, possibly permanently—but if we're lucky, just several months."

Just several months of being attached to a giant machine to clean your blood for you.

Or you die.

Just tubes and pumps and total dependency on foreign technology.

Just a knowing that every three days when you drive to the hospital to get hooked up, it's because you're literally dying, and would die if you stopped the car and waited long enough.

For several agonizing hours, as tubes go into and out of your body, the process is reversed, the ever flowing toxins of life kept at bay, as your body automatically makes more, seemingly unaware it has no place to process them.

"Oh God," my mom said.

We asked more questions. "Yes, he could die."

Now.

Today.

Randomly, in the next several days.

I asked him if he knew if it would what would affect the surgical outcome. He said it depended on the operation and how things went. A few pleasantries, words less significant than me seeing my dad one last time before all this started and him saying "I love you and remember me at my best, not at what you're about to see" and so everything else escaped conscious awareness.

And the doctor left to go back to the OR.

My mom was too out of it for me to have a positive impact on her, and even if she had more composure, I was, for a long moment of incredible nothingness, completely speechless. I think she might have actually gotten up at that point to talk to nurses, to keep her mind occupied so her emotions wouldn't overwhelm—a trait of avoidance I picked up over the years, but one that, if it could be excused at any time, this was one of them.

I picked up my computer, walked away and opened a homework file. That was my own technique for avoidance.

I could tell she wanted me both close by and at a distance. She didn't want me to see her like this, but wanted us to be close together. I felt the same.

I stared at the screen. My brain literally wouldn't function normally. I started looking for things to do—files to delete, documents to open. Figuring out how to access an internet among infinite distraction and popups. The world was a haze.

The avoidance took over. It was me, so powerfully that the fog turned into syrup, covering everything, blurring details in massive static.

A nagging desire to escape the present moment.

I stared at the screen, looked down the hallway. Fluorescent lights. Looked down the waiting room. Fluorescent lights and prime time news on TV—something with the Middle East.

The reporter's voice was a buzz, blended in body parts half-formed words of two dozen comatose family members, all sharing the cold terror of the unknown as strangers on a bus that might or might not crash, as everyone either thought about their next meal or how they could ever eat again, and my legs keep crossing and uncrossing, two cups of instant hot chocolate cooling on the table, and the reporter going on and on, those half-formed words and "The hopes of that man were not in vain" she said, intelligibly—and then more static over the world.

I felt... strange.

I felt, stranger than strange. This feeling, familiar. This knowing, absolute and within. This... stillness.

It's as if my emotions simply turned off, my thoughts ceased, and a completely relaxed stillness, a calmness of being, was all that was present. For a flash of unmeasured and unmeasurable time, there was nowhere to go, and nothing to do. It was the cliche come to life, and in that awareness, it did not matter.

I saw my hand move, my field of vision changed. Without really thinking about it, without really intending it, I knew what to do.

Pretend to journal, so they couldn't tell. A document with many lengthy paragraphs, so anyone watching would think I was doing something normal. I dimmed the screen, and focused on the empty space between the lines.

I thought of my earlier training, between ages twelve to fourteen. I would have felt ridiculously embarrassed to just stand up, cast a circle, call the corners, evoke ancient deities of healing and chant—especially without my incense and crystals.

Everything part of me wanted to do, I realized, sitting within that stillness, in time shorter than it took to read these words—I realized that none of that was necessary.

My mind had 1000 questions, and the part of me that liked to feel smart and say "*this* is the type of Magic that requires no props. They're all just tools for consciousness." The voice of Frick teaching Merlin that the highest level of Magic was the one of pure thought.

Another voice, soft, existing, omnipresent and not coming from any identifiable source: "Let's go."

A gentle push, on the top of my back.

I sat, but no longer stirred. In stillness and knowing, here in my power like it had never been lost, only forgotten. The pilot light was always on, *always on*, for times such as these.

This was who I was at my core. I was not a Wiccan. I was not a Reiki initiate. I was something else, something more. The words didn't matter.

Knowing was reality. Not a hope, a wish, a thought. The knowing was a seeing.

Flashes of images: My dad, well and happily walking around. A clean bill of health. The flow of sparkling healthy fluid, following the natural melodies of the body. His kidneys flowing properly, pumping like organs in a symphony with his bladder, his heart.

No damage. No problems. No life threatening situation.

He is whole.

He is healed.

Simply and completely.

This I intend. This I manifest. This I will.

This is.

In about 33 seconds, it was over. The knowing was my sole and entire identity. It didn't warrant analyzing. I knew what happened as surely as an apple is an apple. My ego returning, a thought arose: "my dad is no longer in jeopardy."

There was no need to re-initiate that incredible feeling, to try and continue. The Work was complete.

I closed my laptop. Stood up. Took a breath. Had some hot chocolate.

Sat. Opened an essay on Developmental Psychology.

This tingling... it wasn't yet time to begin working.

Even though the entire manifestation might have taken less than a minute and it built up to one peak moment – that experience was draining in the sense of running a mental marathon. Or perhaps a spiritual one... I didn't know what to call it. I observed myself, curious to discover changes so dramatic and so rapid.

I knew the feeling...just as releasing certain fluids can temporarily deplete vitality in men, releasing... dare I say it... releasing Magical energy seemed to have temporarily drain something else.

I knew without thinking that it was just like lifting weights, and after a certain recovery period... well, that didn't matter.

Despite the fatigue, my mind kicked up again—somehow this primal reactive part of me hadn't completely shut off, but was just shoved to the side to make room for something greater.

So to avoid it again, I tried to review my psych notes and looked over to check in on mom, and the elevator door opened again with the same doctor. Mom got anxious and started to freak, but in that same instant, the Reptile in my brain ceased, and the stillness returned. And I knew with calm clarity that things were fine.

"How is he? How's he doing? Is he alright? What happened? Did he... is he...?" she said in hobbling rapid fire.

"He's actually doing a lot better," the doctor said. "We're sewing him up. We'll put him on dialysis for a few hours to be safe, but his kidneys started working properly approximately five minutes ago. Based on how they are now, he almost definitely won't need dialysis for months. I don't know what happened, but it seemed like his body just kicked into gear. To follow protocol, we're going to monitor him closely for a few days, but I don't expect anything serious."

The shock on mom's face had been replaced with confusion. So sudden and pure, that space when reality shifts and the next logical step doesn't happen.

She was worrying about and expecting something so opposite, it was as if her system didn't believe him, couldn't allow relief after so much danger. She kept asking questions for confirmation. They continued talking, the compassionate physician and the disbelieving bystander.

"Thank you," I said. Our eyes met. Mine were calm and happy; his were the carefully controlled, neutral expression of a physician. Mom was in good hands, and wanted to fulfill her curiosity. There was nothing more I needed to know.

I rose and walked away for more hot chocolate.

12

Faith

"Faith is taking the first step, even when you don't see the whole staircase."

-*King*

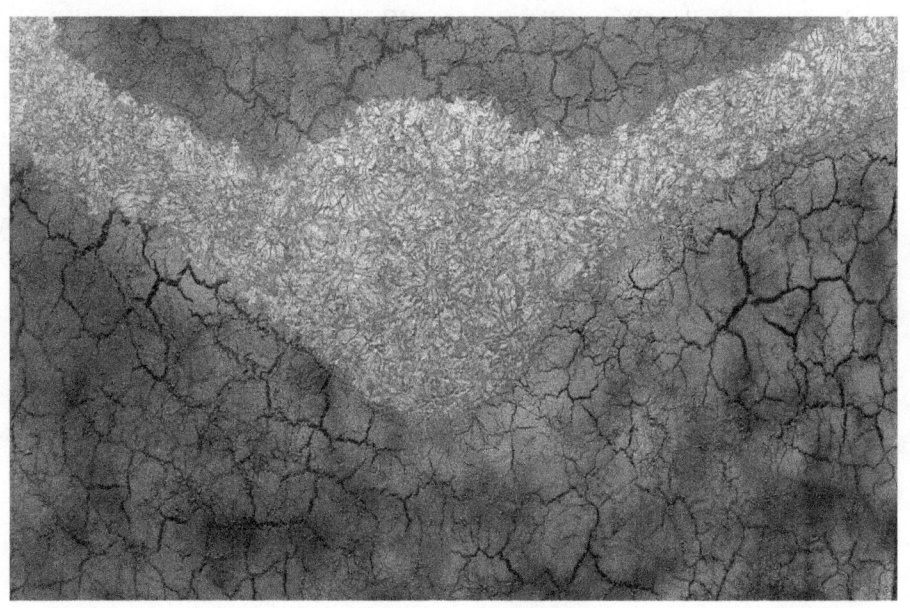

Expectation creates reality.
Expectation requires faith.

Expectation followed by a result other than what you expected shows you your attachments.

Opportunities to release attachments are a chance to become a fraction more freer, a fraction more enlightened, a fraction more magically powerful.

Sometimes, what you asked for or what you wished for will supersede an expectation. This is true at the highest esoteric levels and in basic legal contracts. If someone you consider trustworthy says that they will "Not torture you" and "Not kill you," and some bizarre circumstance occurs where they must torture you for a bearable time in order to not kill you... logic clearly shows that the higher action, the superior outcome, mattered more than the specifics of any one element in the equation.

Such is the same in life. In any day, week, month or year, the "gift" of suffering may be the key that unlocks the door. You can always avoid a scary, unpleasant or undesirable key... but at some level if you expected a door to have a certain type of key, you must wield it, and you must use it, in order to walk through.

The same is true with the quest for new keys. Is it possible? Is there a cost? Is there a road, significantly longer than the path already in front of you? Is there more mystery, and thus possibly more risk?

Let's not get lost in philosophy. The answer, a simple sentence, would be easy to type, easy to share. How you find the best keys to the best door, the effort and cost, the time and the outcome... all of these are available to you at all times.

Rather than give you that sentence, I shall give you a series of experiences. Everything you encounter that I create, every chapter, every interaction. Quite possibly, moments in your life, the hand that is Unity existing, seen and unseen, behind certain events, certain circumstances.

A direct transmission of the "Mystery" in mystery schools. If the sentence comes to you intuitively, in your own words of truth and consistency, of stillness and effectiveness... Mazel Tov!

Until it does—and until it solidifies, you can still learn about faith. So here is the rest of the chapter, as much as you believe you need it.

I never thought "faith" would be part of my life. It always seemed like something ignorant people did. Faith was an activity, not a state of being.

Being. What was that, even?

My friend Tom, a lucky 23-year-old millionaire who made his fortune in robotics that optimized solar arrays, once said something so critical I wanted to tattoo it on my right wrist.

He said, "just be."

Somehow, despite hearing that on a spiritual retreat, and Tom is not super spiritual... somehow knowing someone, respecting them... envying them... made their words stick more.

But being was something that was foreign to me. I don't know why... Like a perpetual test I kept getting a "D" grade on, despite consistently taking and retaking it... in scenarios like this, you realize that you never learned how to study, never knew what to study.

So "Being faithful" was just as foreign a concept as "Being still." I had no idea what it meant intellectually or was like experientially.

Fast forward in time. An old familiar, Boo (a delightful 26-foot tall Astral doggie represented in the body of an adorable stuffed animal), told me to start writing, until 9:45 pm, right around 9:14. And it's... it's not foreign at all, trusting that part of myself that I personify as him (and also IS him, depending on the level of awareness).

Trust is something that's also new. I remember buying The Courage to Trust, a book with the cover of two hands, one holding the other. One sleeve red, the other one gray. I remember really knowing I needed that book, and only being able to vaguely admit to myself that the reason why was because Trust was such a foreign concept.

The betrayal from a past life that contributed to this is a topic for another story. Suffice to say, the fact I can trust an inner/intuitive voice now, and have faith that the guidance was legit and the actions have merit... is pretty awesome!

Our minds aren't made to take us all the way to the Infinite. They exist to take us about three-quarters of the way there. Most of us aren't aware of our minds as individual entities (programs?)—but when you begin to meditate deeply and consistently, and fully feel yourself as The Witness, you embody the truth that you are not your thoughts.

And recognizing this, that your thoughts come from somewhere and that You exist independently... that leads to, if you keep exploring, the realization that you are a soul.

This process continues in the same fractalkine way. Just as a lower awareness of "I am the mind" is "I am the body", the higher awareness of "I am the soul" is also just a stepping stone. "I am part of the Oversoul" and "I am the Oversoul" and "I am divine in a collective of beings who are also divine" to eventually the flash of awareness that "I am God"—very few of us truly get there, in an embodied way.

Touching that—touching true Unity—is when Miracles happen. At that moment of unification, there is no time or space or separation. Miracles simply "Are."

Yet to perceive them, the unfolding of the event where rain falls at your command, or the wound heals, or the plant grows at rapid speed, you have to view from time and thus are farther from Unity, the observer and no longer the doer, and the object itself.

So how to shift from thought and mind to soul, and how to shift from Soul to God?

I could tell you... but before we go further... do you trust me?

Do you trust this experience?

You know your answer because it existed at a subtle level. If you could feel that answer and it was "Yes," then there you are. A signpost of intuition, of awareness of knowledge beyond thought. A breadcrumb, an arrow, towards your own God/Self-realization.

If "no", then likely you either had confusion, or stopped to think, and made a decision. If this is the case...

Where did you lose it, and how do you rebuild it?

An event in this life, when you were young, related to your parents or primary caregivers?

Something traumatic, that affected how you saw the world?

Or it could be something from a close friend or teacher - some powerful experience where trust was broken, and you never fully recovered?

This is a book of instruction and transmutation... it is not a book, explicitly about healing. If you want to heal so you can truly, deeply, fully Trust again, I recommend the books *Codependent No More* by Melody Beattie, *The Celestine Prophecy* by James Redfield, and *The Law of Attraction* by Hicks, along with other methods you feel deep down will work, and will repair this aspect of you, related to your Second Chakra.

If you have access to an excellent somatic therapist, consider looking into attachment theory, and how to restore secure attachment.

Sometimes, if the wound is great, the idea of trust can evoke great fear.

Because faith requires trust in the divine, and faith, as it is applied to Magic, is required to manifest, and fear is a powerful gravity force, you may wish to consider this topic extremely thoroughly.

This is an initiation into radical honesty and self-awareness.

Faith is not stupidity, nor is it ignorance or delusion, hope or belief.

Stepping off a cliff because you *want* to fly is not faith, no matter how much you use the word. Faith is the blurry bridge between Belief and Knowledge, both of which are above Hope.

Faith is like a muscle. The more you use it, the more you understand it. The stronger and easier it becomes, and the more often and more accurately it works.

Faith is that thing you felt when you read the first part of this chapter, of inferior quality to the writing here, and maintained your focus, read without abnormal interruption, because you knew without *physical* validation (the validation was psychic) that the chapter would get better.

Everything. Is. Intentional.

Bwahaha!

Congratulations. Whether you "succeeded" or "failed" at the above test, now you're here. You're farther than you would have been otherwise. Regardless of your level of faith, *you now have a direct embodied experience of it.*

Possibly your faith in me/this book was strong. Perhaps it was weak. Perhaps you quantify it at 58.2% and don't know what to call it. Average?

Like the shade of gray of concrete or the typically standard size of jeans or people who talk without thinking or eye contact or the fact we are polluting the world and not healing her quality enough because it's quicker to watch television and gratify instead of finding and living a higher ambition but who really cares because this is a run on sentence are you bored or excited or picking up my airs I mean errors what is even happening here?

A second triangle elephant snake tooth. Just the first letters of those last four words, because to say the word would give it away to your peripheral vision and the purpose of these two paragraphs would have been compromised.

Did you think, "This chapter has gotten better, but now it's way worse! I feel let down"?

Did you think, "This is awesome. I have no idea what he's trying to say or why he's cramming several ideas into one long chunk and making some of the simplest mistakes a writer can make, but I just know there's a higher purpose behind it?"

Did your faith lower, or rise?

Such is what happens when our faith is tested.

Learned Helplessness is a psychology term meaning "I don't think it's worthwhile to try again, because last time trying this went so poorly."

The technical definition on Apple's Dictionary app as of May 2018 is "A condition in which a person suffers from a sense of powerlessness, arising from a traumatic event or persistent failure to succeed. It is thought to be one of the underlying causes of depression."

Power. Less.

Is your Magical power compromised by your lack of faith, in yourself or the universe?

Has ridicule, scorn, or trauma affected your ability to hope for a better future?

Have you ever given up before you truly began? Before you legitimately assessed a situation's chances of success and all the routes you could take to succeed?

HOLOGRAPHIC FAITH

This Book as a Hologram of Life

Using this book as an example, think of all you have read, all you have learned. Think of what felt right, and what felt true. That which felt useful, and that which felt... less useful.

The stuff that felt right immediately was what you naturally digested.

That which felt less useful... was it because you didn't see how it was immediately relevant?

Because you didn't believe it?

Because you wanted it communicated in a different way, with more examples, detail, or exercises?

Those parts are a test of your faith.

Can you consider one of those parts, and shift to a *trusting* that the benefits, while possibly not immediately apparent, will become so when you need them most?

Do you need the word "could" instead of "will" in the above sentence to make it easier?

Do you feel, deep down, how a "yes" to the above question is a lower degree of faith to the vibration of certainty that accompanies "will?"

"This could happen" means you believe in a possibility, or perhaps hope for it.

"This will happen" means you have faith. There is a knowing before physical validation.

In a 3D restricted world, the probability isn't definite, for any number of reasons. Meteors could hit. Bombs could explode. People could die, or interfere.

In a 9D unity reality, all worlds of all possibilities exist simultaneously. Your *perfect* level of non-attachment from want (fear, desire) is what prevents the undesired outcome from manifesting. How well you direct your intention, *feel yourself in the reality you wish for*—this is what raises the probability of "This will happen."

And when you know, truly and deeply, that the "will" contains certainty, as close to 100% as can be, then your Faith has evolved to Knowing.

And that, my fellow Magician, is a core—if not the *core*—mechanic of Magic.

EXERCISE: MAINTAINING FAITH IN THE FACE OF FAILURE

Consider 5 things that you believe *will* occur within the next week, and five things that have a high probability of successfully occurring. Let's ignore, for now, the bizarre circumstances of spontaneous combustion and explosions. Let's exist in the regular world, with things occurring as they normally do.

Pick things that you assess the probability at greater than 84%.
Write them each down, summarized in one sentence. Write out the level of likelihood they have of occurring as you describe them.

Pick items that have a clear "yes or no." If there were several conditions, use a probability for each. It's better to have 5 things as general "yes" or "no" options than get into so much detail that you have 20 sub-probabilities for each item. Let's keep it simple and avoid overthinking.

Set a reminder to return to this exercise in a week, and review your list.

Now do the same with 5 things you believe *might* occur, i.e. a probability of 65-83%.

Repeat this for 5 things that *could* occur, at 37-64%.

Lastly, write 5 things that *probably won't* occur, at less than 37%.

Take your list of 20 items. Have it clean and clear, like:

WILL HAPPEN

I will get paid on time: 97%

I will sleep at least 6 nights this week: 93%
(Etc.)

MIGHT HAPPEN

I might experience at least three moments when I feel happy enough to smile spontaneously: 81%

Something will make me laugh unexpectedly: 67%

I might feel motivated to start a new project (72%)
(Etc.)

COULD HAPPEN

I could be disciplined enough to maintain my convictions for a new habit, and perform it exactly as intended with the focus, duration and depth as designed (50%)

I could receive a call from a friend inviting me to a type of event I've wanted to go to (43%)
(Etc.)

PROBABLY WON'T HAPPEN

I probably won't materialize a cat, levitate it, and make it fart sprinkles (2%)

I probably won't start and finish writing that book I've always wanted to write, in the span of 10 days. (7%)

(Etc.)

Consider this list, and consider your belief in yourself for each line item. Did giving a grounded appraisal for each item inspire you to consider the variables which could raise the probability?

Did you have faith in yourself that you could change your life circumstances, and do things that would inspire more friends to call, or more elements to support you being in total and perfect flow for that book to get written?

Since Manifestation is related to altering probabilities, are you starting to see how your ability to manifest depends on your faith in yourself, and the conditions you believe must be necessary to elevate that faith?

What if, for example, none of the conditions for you writing that book were met—but you had total, complete, 100% faith in yourself? Would the conditions matter less?

HOMEWORK

As you review your list, save the following instructions and re-evaluate everything in one week:

Write a "Yes" on the side of everything that happened according to your prediction (reversed for the "won't happen) and a "No" for the opposite.

Then, answer each of these with a journal entry:

Consider deeply your No-s. How did they make you feel? Did they raise or lower your faith *in yourself*?

Consider deeply your Yes-es. Did they strengthen your faith in some way? Yourself, other people, divine providence?

Was there any item that was a "Yes" and, instead of raising your faith, you attributed it to luck or circumstance?

By doing this experiment, and considering each item, you will learn how, at an intimate level, faith operates in your system.

You may discover subtle beliefs, patterns and thoughts behind your faith, what lowers it and what raises it.

With this and any other exercise, what you receive is proportional what you invest.

Faith is more like sub-knowledge, a certainty of something before it is in your material experience. Faith is built slowly when we act in little ways that have no logical reason for turning out in a surprisingly positive fashion. When we take what to others may be perceived as a risk, but to us, if done with sincerity and gratitude, are investments that get paid back with interest. The more we invest, the greater the return.

So what's the difference between walking off the cliff and levitating, versus falling to our deaths?

Sometimes our faith in the spiritual reality rises as a surprise gift.

One day in Italy, I attended Damanhur's Festival of the Dead. I knew somehow that there would be at least one occurrence of overt Magic. Since I had never been to this event since Magic (wow, a super loud spontaneous noise just as I wrote that word! Yay synchronistic signpost!)—since Magic is often unpredictable.

This is the key Esther Hicks alluded to, the key to how the Law of Attraction works. Jerry, her husband, asked, "How can you get in a state of knowing something before you see physical proof?"

She said, "It's just something you'll have to figure out."

Because even though I can tell you about the gust of wind that shook branches on all the nearby trees during the part of the ceremony when the names of the dead (Including Falco,

Damanhur's founder) were spoken, the trees were still the entire time before and after (a span of almost three hours)—to me, this was Magic enough. I didn't need flying translucent spirits or beams of light streaking down from the heavens.

I also noticed the sky that night.

Despite having a healing surgical wound that made it painful to walk, despite being cold, despite the tail end of a rather intense fast. None of these things bothered me. I was calm and content, looking forward to and grateful for the physically visible Magic that occurred.

And the fact it occurred with hundreds of people around, all who witnessed and pointed and smiled... Validation!

It's experiences like these that can build your faith. A purist of some traditions might say we don't need these experiences, and a fundamentalist of others might call them distraction... but I say *Magic is the natural phenomena of divine embodiment.*

It's God winking at you.

And Magic occurs more strongly from *not wanting or needing* the payoff, lest you strengthen egoic attachments that take you farther down the continuum of enlightenment.

Faith need not be absolute to "work;" I didn't demonstrate mastery; I *wanted* Magic, and I got it. If I was able to detach more fully... Maybe I would have seen the lights and spirits more strongly.

Just like a filter in channeling... what we can experience is often related to how much "we" as an ego can let go and get out of the way...

Of all the times when I chanted mantras to Lakshmi, the days when the most spiritual/financial returns on investment came were when I really put my soul into it... when I was really, truly devoted. Ten minutes of completely devoted effort, as opposed to multi-tasking and saying mantras while doing laundry or walking Arrow, our cute part German Shepherd, part Wolf doggie.

Grow the muscle. Re-read this chapter, investing your essence and focus and concentration. Have faith you will get *some* valuable benefit from this activity that you otherwise wouldn't have received.

If the deepest, most evolving and revelatory text fell into your lap at the hands of a dirty, smelly stranger covered in rags... would you give that text the same attention as if the Dalai Lama came into the room, looked you deeply into your eyes, and handed you the papers, saying "This is especially relevant for you?"

Sometimes, what we receive is what we are able to receive.

Sometimes, all that really matters is the one sentence that sticks in our minds, and all the rest is filler.

Expecting a poetic, philosophical chapter on faith in order to help you grow your faith is like expecting your muscles to grow bigger before they lift the weights.

Sometimes, the change needs to happen inside you.

Sometimes, you just have to be willing.

Sometimes, diamonds really are in the ruff.

You decide... or you already know.

Feel, as your faith is honored and grows, the possibility for real Magic to occur immediately, to your benefit and your awakening.

Do so now. Look deep into your core. What is there? What do you feel you need? Can you let that, too, go?

Congratulations, for the effort you did invest. Even seriously considering my offer for a fraction of a second was a demonstration of your innate faith.

You can only go up from here.

13
The Future of Magic

"The best way to predict the future is to create it."

-Abraham Lincoln, Peter Drucker and Steve Jobs

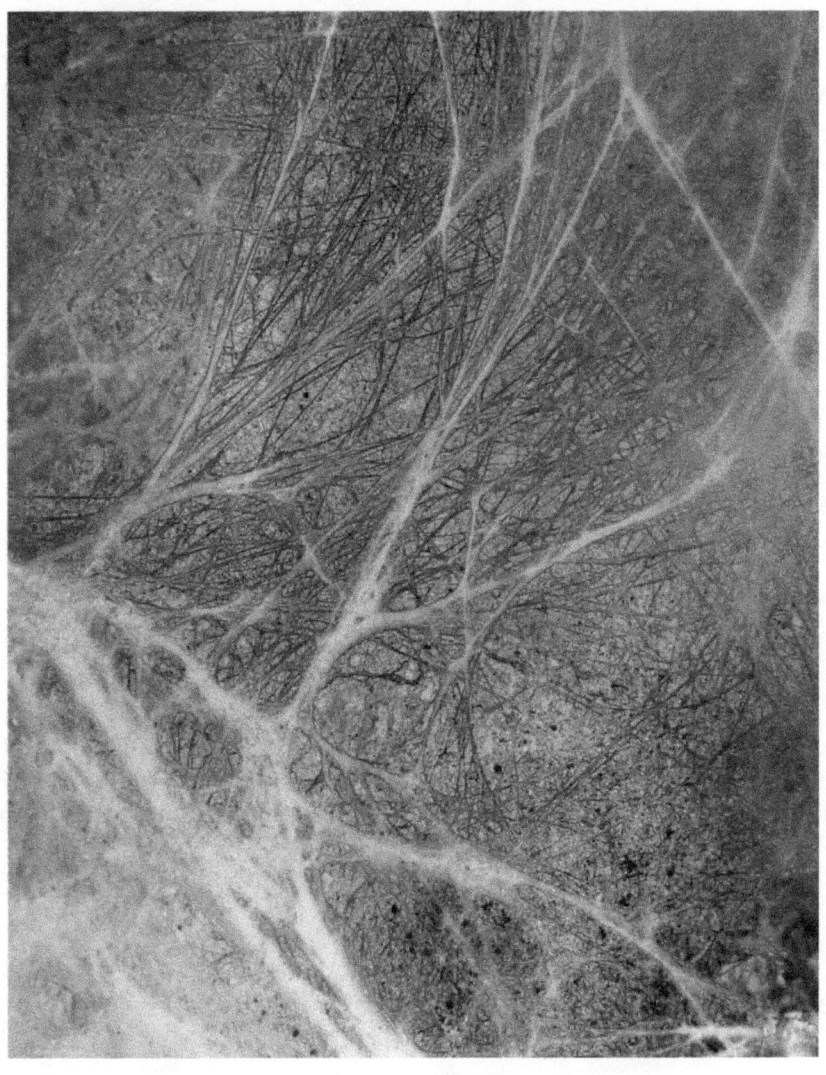

The work of this collective is just beginning. Magic is Real is a 7-book series, with future books covering a variety of topics that include:

- Guided practices to open your third eye
- A growing list of validated miracles
- Scientific references and highlights from many researchers
- Detailed instructions on how to perform specific techniques like clairvoyance, telekinesis, weather control, precognition, channeling, telepathy and Elemental Magic

You will also receive deeper explorations into the science of enlightenment based on an examination of techniques from leading researchers in the field. For the most general, concise, scientific purposes, the systems of enlightenment we will explore have an analytical focus. There's a lot of poetry about this loaded term, and we will help deconstruct, demystify and describe the components of it in a way you can digest.

Overall, enlightenment can be seen as a stepping stone and not an end goal. It is not something which requires you to leave society, drastically change your life, or have white halos floating around you all the time. It is, at its most basic, a state of awareness allowing you to see yourself as a soul and a state of psychology absent of emotional reactivity.

Described in this way, enlightenment can come and go. It's a continuum rather than an end point, and is only as special as you allow it to be. Just like being in great athletic shape, being on the enlightenment spectrum enables you to experience life a certain way, but it doesn't make you superior to other people. Rather, it's a certain freedom—and just like maintaining your physical fitness, often you'll need to perform practices to maintain the level of enlightenment you are able to reach.

The biggest thing enlightenment helps with is a level of non-attachment, which is a key ingredient to manifestation, which we have already written about extensively and will be discussed in multiple chapters of future books.

The first sequel to this book will contain more stories and techniques on Flashy Magic, Channeling and biographical stories of powerful Magicians. You will have the opportunity to learn about Breatharianism (how to live off Prana) by a leader of the field.

In print and online, we'll cover Money Magic, a glossary of spiritual terms, and will provide a greater emphasis on exercises and techniques so you can apply this knowledge directly into your life.

One of the seven books will contain more epic Magic battles and transmissions through fiction, describing a future possible world with all the intensity of a good story. We'll go into a future Atlantis, a Magical city, and explore the astral realm more deeply, starting with a chapter called How to Meet Your Spirit Guide.

Books are just the beginning, an introductory point to a much larger mission. Through text, video and digital communities, we will continually invite you to participate in creating a future world, a Magical Golden Age that humanity is ready for.

This is a practical chapter outlining actions in the material world, and so is organized thus, by topic. Additional ways you can be involved with the Magic is Real community are to receive:

1. **Updates on Magical discoveries:**

    Education, research, and events (both digital and physical) via newsletters at <u>MagicalGoldenAge.com</u>. On our site you will also find an archive of interviews, videos, and previews for upcoming books.

2. **Magical Mastermind:**

    12 weeks to spiritual flourishing. This is a digital curriculum that includes homework, a buddy system, and Q&A designed to support your evolution and training. This is an all-encompassing upgrade for key aspects of your life, to free you of perceived restrictions in the material realm, and support your optimal health. We will teach you how to free yourself of karmic and energetic blocks and transition into a lifestyle of continuous and radiant joy.

Mastermind topics include:

- Initiation into Unity Magic
- Lifestyle recommendations to purify your mind, body, and spirit
- Guidelines for optimal nutrition, supplements, and exercise
- Overview and training in specific mystical abilities, with live exercises and activations
- Past life healings, trauma clearing exercises, and neurological reprogramming techniques
- Psychic Defense skills
- Manifestation techniques
- Group rituals and spells to amplify our focus and energies
- Live channeling of angels, star people, and divine beings
- Retreats at spiritual sites around the world, where we can practice High Magic and attend both healing and training immersions for deep, comprehensive and rapid spiritual development

3. **Monthly group rituals:**

   Combine your intentions and efforts with many beings around the world. Collective intent amplifies Magical power and healing energies and can manifest significantly greater changes than solitary work. The topics will rotate, and there will be a voting system where participants can request and support specific topics.

4. **Magical Experiments:**

   Imagine a world where over 1000 people collectively send Loving energies to plants in controlled laboratory conditions, and the growth of the plants is recorded. How much faster can a plant grow if it has the support of 5 Magicians, compared to 50 and 500?

How could the world shift if this data could be replicated and expanded upon to regrow forests, reform glaciers and heal ecosystems?

What if the same format were used in healing, reducing the recovery time of major injuries and illnesses by 30, 60 and 90 percent? What formulas and combinations could make healing instant? How could this be explained using 3D (Mind-body / Placebo), 4D (Astral-Energetic) and 5D (Causal-Karmic) models?

What could happen if 10, 100 or 1000 people all focused on you, sending you the intention you need most? Could this help accelerate the development of clairvoyant abilities? Could this enhance your access to rich, divine embodiment? Could this turn your life around financially much faster than you ever anticipated?

Could we all focus our chi in an array to produce visible light around a crystal?

I once achieved this in a small group. We saw several visible sparks, and a light bluish-white glow around the piece of quartz I had been charging for over a year. How many Magicians would it take, working together, to replicate this effect—consistently and on camera?

Let's find out.

What if we could help populations of homeless, abused or mentally challenged people who are willing to receive Loving support? The Maharishi Effect has been documented to lower crime in areas where large numbers of meditators focus. We can build upon this and change the world through consistent, coordinated prayer.

Massive energies are coming into our field of awareness, increasing as each of us awaken incrementally on a day to day basis. The collective efforts of many can accomplish much more than the individual efforts of a few. Let's actively build the world of the golden age now.

We Magicians may be spread out across the world, but with the barriers of time and space removed thanks to digital and psychic tools, the opportunities to impact our planet, our people, and our galaxy in a radiant way have never been so great.

5. **The Wall of Miracles**:

   Imagine a collection of miraculous happenings that shows up as a wall of inspiring videos. Like many sites that host videos, the Wall of Miracles could be sorted by category, like valuable synchronicity, precognition, materialization, teleportation, or other highly Magical moments.

This would be a way you could share your progress with the world, and learn from fellow Magicians who are developing similar skills. Just like we can see expert gymnasts online, it's time we see expert Magicians on demand!

The great feats of masters in Qigong, Telekinesis, Spiritual Healing and other examples of Applied Consciousness on YouTube vary greatly in their quality, clarity and instruction. A good database linked to detailed instructions could de-mystify mysticism, and enable everyone to see what's possible as we awaken to our true nature.

6. **Wikipedia of Open Sourced Magic**:

   What if we could build a database that links together all the Magical systems of the world? This would include Hermetics, Kaballah, Christian Science, Tarot, Druidism, Qigong, Tai Chi, Chaos Magick, Wicca, Yogic Siddhis, and many lesser known yet very effective mystery traditions? We could draw parallels between each, and safely categorize practices into protected levels of initiations to ensure a safe transmission.

What if we could look at how every religion talked about prophecy, clairvoyance, animal communication and spiritual healing, and could figure out what's most effective? Discern the optimal methods to build these abilities as quickly and safely as possible?

We could examine all the references to sacred geometry, numerology, and astrology and find the common threads. We could see what each system says about correspondences, diet, altered states of consciousness, working with spirits and other matters, and drill deeper into the mechanisms of action, the similarities, the differences—essentially, we can optimize Magic!

Just like the traditional Wikipedia, this project may take time to become saturated with high quality references and will need many volunteers to help maintain accuracy, thoroughness, and validity.

Whether a complete organization of the world's Magical systems takes two years or ten, the benefits will be vast. For the first time in modern history, we can finally have a compilation of Magic knowledge as we do for nutrition and fitness.

Perhaps someday we could even create a safe AI like the IBM Watson of Magic.

"Siri, levitate that cat!"

"Cortana, teleport me to the beach!"

"Alexa, I'm ready for my next telepathy lesson!"

And why shouldn't we levitate cats, so long as Mr Kitty enjoys it? As useful and practical as Magic can be, we enjoy the taste bud-transforming miracle fruit and the thrilling movements of dance. We have fun with our bodies, and play with our minds.

Having fun with Magic is a natural result of raising our capabilities to the level where we are fluent. While it might be unwise to experiment with the source code of reality on the fly (and thus turn a literal fly into a literal Saber-tooth Tiger), realizing the truth of our nature as infinite beings playing in a world of illusion may as well include the perks of enjoying that illusion. It doesn't all have to be super serious stuff.

Since that technology will undoubtedly become available at some point in time, a strong argument can be made to first ensure its development in the hands of compassionate and Loving beings of service. With the rise of quantum computing, one could even say this is a time sensitive priority worthy of a significant budget.

Contributing in whatever way feels aligned is thus both a way to spread Magic throughout the world, and ensure that, by the time we can cast them, there are protective grids preventing renegade Magicians from materializing alligators in your bed before you wake up.

Stuffed unicorns with poetic messages tied to their horns? Now that's worth considering.

7. **Another way you can get more deeply involved is by requesting Personal Magical Training and healing:**

    David Solomon and Certified Magicians schedule regular availability to help students clear energetic and karmic blocks, heal emotional wounds, and create personal Magical Development Paths.

We all have gifts, and the approach of finding a fellow student to be *friendtors* with (friend + mentor, geddit?) is golden. If you don't have the budget to hire a professional or otherwise prefer to trade sessions, you could submit your information into our Magical Matchmaking service and be paired up with someone who has energy healing, soul embodiment, past life regression and other skills they can offer.

Just like in schools of massage therapy, it's very helpful to have the opportunity to practice with another student as you refine your skills. The best way to ensure the abilities you need are available when you need them is to actively use them, and teaming up with a fellow Magician can be a great way to do this.

Whether you practice with someone from the Magic is Real network or someone you meet in the world at large, here are a few guidelines for each person to consider:

- Do you come from service, in support of each other's highest spiritual evolution?

- Do you or they have subtle abilities that could influence the other person? Just like a well-trained salesperson can direct conversations according to her preferences, it's ethical to be fully transparent about each other's abilities, and to always honor consent.

Just like an ethical salesperson serves the role of a consultant, offering without striving to persuade, an ethical spiritual guide should do the same.

Words only mean what we choose for them to mean. Traditions exist because we allow them to persist. We can also examine them, reboot them, and redefine the m.

Always remember: Waking up and Growing up!

- Know where are both of you on your various learning curves. Find clear, mutually agreeable standards to assess and measure the abilities at hand. Several guides for these purposes will be published in future MIR books.

Understand, and be radically honest with each other, related your developmental stages for all related topics. This can take up to two hours for looking deep into both the Waking Up (spiritual awakening to your true nature as a being of infinite potential) and Growing Up (psychological maturity to act responsibly based on the world and people around you).

Long term partnerships between fellow students should have check-ins to confirm where each person is at. While eventually we will release software to quickly discern this, for now, be aware of as much as you can—and at the very least, be transparent about "spikes," or transitions from the norm.

For example, is person A stably Grown Up except related to concepts related to her father, which trigger her? Is person B stably Woken Up to have very high levels of psychic abilities, except related to the topics of physical bodies, where he has wounds and karmic-perceptual blocks?

In these cases, the pair would best be served not working too deeply on topics related to fathers or bodies, unless there is good support present, or a high level of validated skill in one of the individuals.

We are, all of us, always growing and learning. In the infinite multiverse of Unity, there is only one awareness at a given moment that is the strongest, most knowledgeable, most skilled, most infallible consciousness to exist.

While in every moment of now that is potentially you, in most moments of now, your experience is what it is. If you perceive yourself—or others perceive you—as a being who is constantly transforming and "leveling up," learning and unlearning, growing and evolving, then be aware of this fact.

Forgive yourself. Ask others to forgive you. Do your best in every moment. Commit this. Ask for others to do the same.

Be straightforward about how resourced you are. Do you have the capacity to continue, if in session? Are you able to hold space and be nonjudgmental, Lovingly supportive, and meet your partner where they are at?

Trigger topics, biochemistry, environment, people and so many factors can take us up or down the Awaken and Grown scales, at any time. Any being or master could (or could be perceived to be) at a very high level one moment, then not, the next.

While stability is usually constant, be aware of this fact. Your inner truth—the sober, consistent blend of creative / logical, masculine / feminine, light / dark, east / west, electric / magnetic, heavenly / earthly oneness that you seek to embody in every moment... seek first to know thyself, thy baseline, and thy range.

If you could quantify any of these aspects on a scale of 0-100, where do you usually exist? 40-60? 80-90? 14-77 in wide swings?

Just like an ideal diet is customized based on your activity levels and other factors, an ideal session should take into context the complexity of your life.

As you shift from the thinking ego-mind to the knowing soul-awareness, this knowing will get easier, and eventually become instant.

Just as when you unearth a potted plant to examine its growth, doing so (and meticulously analyzing yourself) can stunt or even kill the plant if overdone.

Therefore, seek, measure, consider... and be reasonable.

- Another factor to consider in Magical Practice Sessions: Is there a mature, experienced person who can supervise, review, and help plan the training?
- Constantly encourage and support each other, while being honest about what you perceive and experience. Stay positive, optimistic, and over everything else, embody a Loving and compassionate attitude.
- If you take the role of a healer, you are absolutely in dedication to the other being. Especially if you do not yet have certification, training and the recommendation of an experienced teacher, you must remember that your client / healee is the boss, and in charge of their own session, actions, and pacing. Never force anyone to do anything they don't feel aligned to do.
- Mind altering substances are discussed in greater detail in future books. While they can be attractive, and while there are ways to find pure substances, bless them, and take them with reverence in a healthy set and setting, we don't recommend them.
- Many people have reported access to clairvoyant and other abilities via plant medicines and drugs...and many people have experienced life-altering side effects that outweigh the benefits such substances provide. While it might feel good to get a flash of insight, a flood of dopamine and serotonin, and an abundance of DMT to

help you see the spirit world, all these phenomena can occur naturally—and far more sustainably—with good training.

- If you are ever in a position of power, meaning someone trusts you to direct their actions in a practice, healing or training session, you must only use this power in dedication to the light.

As written elsewhere, we hereby bind every being encountering these teachings from committing any harmful, subversive or controlling acts against another soul that affects that soul in a way which causes suffering, alignment to lack, or a doubt in their divine nature; any Magical action taken in this way will be stripped of power, and any Magician seeking to cause this (including you, if this applies) will be similarly reduced in awareness and access to abilities until a full and complete atonement is made.

At that point, the road to restore awareness and power will be permanently steeper, with more safeguards, supervision, and Divine intercession accepted as part of the atonement process to safeguard our people and our planet.

All those of you who receive this section and offer a personalized vow of agreement, from your heart, will have earned a level of trust, and thus merit a frequency of blessing, not given to those who do not. If you wish to offer such a vow, do so now, with complete focus and conviction.

These precautions are essential. While our culture is evolving and certain practices that used to be taboo are slowly gaining acceptance, everyone matures at a different rate, and some activities (like sexual activities) should be held with the utmost sacredness and reverence.

The benefits of living in a digital age include transparency and achievability. Ultimately, all of your actions can become known, both psychically and physically.

You should feel free and encouraged to learn, grow, and realize that we all mature at a certain rate. We're all born pooping our pants, and we all learn everything as we go. Failure to act in the way we choose to act when we are more experienced does not mean that failure was intentional... that being said, with any words or actions you perform Magically, affecting the consciousness of other beings, act as if your behaviors and innermost intentions were known, fully and completely, to both your guides and the world at large.

Consider, possibly, making certain promises, covenants, and agreements. Consider getting these agreements on video with anyone you choose to work with. And consider the fact that we all share the same world, that life is long, and that you may want to enrich and be enriched by the people you encounter for decades to come.

Shortcuts to pleasure almost never go well. There are some powerful tools we are giving you and have given you, and ultimately it is your responsibility to be aware of the maturity, awareness and intent of both yourself and any partner. Be they an academic or any other type of partner, consider your higher self—your highest self—and act accordingly.

Karma is real.

So too is forgiveness.

And, just like in earlier chapters, consider sending anyone those energies now. If you feel someone wronged you or you wronged someone else (defining "wrong" as any action that doesn't serve the highest self), come clean. Every day is judgment day, and every moment we are creating our own unique heaven or metaphorical hell. We can transition between these states in the snap of a finger, and heaven—in all forms and all definitions—is always open to you.

Working with a professional teacher is of course a way to raise the probability that your time will be used wisely, that you will learn at a quick pace, and that you will be in good hands. If you and a friend want to train together, hiring a coach can also help you support each other, so you can be economically mindful and have an independent third party confirm everything spoken here.

Some ideas are worth repeating. Any teacher, healer, or spiritual support person who lives in the material world must be supported as such. Not all of us can live off Prana and not need to buy food. It is completely acceptable to exchange the energy of Money for the energy of time and effort; this does not "muddy" a spiritual concept in the least.

As with Magical Masterminds, personal training professionally provided by the Magic is Real network is an expenditure of energy and an offering that most beings take more seriously with an energetic exchange. To support these efforts, along with the building of temples and construction of Atlantis Reborn, scholarships and work trades will be available to those who can contribute in meaningful ways to these projects and who do not have the funds to engage financially.

Much has been said about the blending of energies of spirituality and money. While these are often steeped in judgment, for millennia donations have been provided to spiritual services.

By attaching financial models to Magical training, we hope to make these skills "normal" as the economy transitions and more "mainstream" jobs are outsourced to artificial intelligence and professionally directed robots.

To honor the life of every individual, we will constantly provide opportunities for you to be involved in ways other than through financial energies.

However, as always, honor your own truth. If it feels appropriate to you to only receive training, healing and support from those who do not need or request the energy of money for their services, honor that path, wherever it leads you. There is room for everything in Unity, and every expression is as Divine, blessed and reverent as you choose to see it to be.

8. **Live Demos of Flashy Magic. Traditionally, only a small minority of people have demonstrated feats like:**

- Levitation (Tibetan and other lineages, accessible after years of practice)
- Creating fire with chi
- Rapid healing of wounds and the knitting together of flesh
- Vanishing of tumors recorded on Ultrasound and shared digitally (See Gregg Braden's videos)
- The manifestation of visible light around a human body (Ron Holman, Alain Forget)
- Rapid growth of plants, such as in the rainforest regeneration by the Kogi people in the 2012 movie Aluna.

Our abilities and skills as human beings often exist in bell curves:

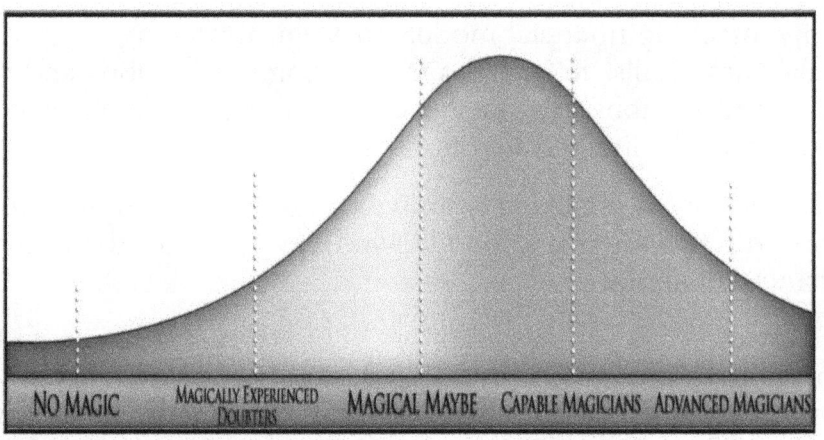

Only a small number of people exist in the far right section as "Extremely Advanced." These individuals often show early access to high levels of mystical abilities early in life and are more likely to become gurus, famous healers, and overall Magical badasses. They come from many walks of life, of many traditions and cultures, and often choose paths and careers immersed in spiritual life.

A larger number of people are in the "Accelerated Growth" track, born with a higher than average potential to access Magical abilities. These individuals may have periods where they experience more common occurrences of spiritual and mystical phenomena, such as precognition, psychic traits, ability to manipulate the weather, and energy healing skills. Most of these beings need training, and some are referred to as Crystalline or Indigo children.

Of course, the opposites are also true. Some people on the far left have "No Magic" and are hyper-logical and unable to perceive the spiritual realms and remain, diehard skeptics, their entire life. This is due to both a mix of neural patterning and simply their soul's expression of that sliver of Unity.

The second to the lowest group is "Magically Experienced Doubters," people who may have experienced Magic and recognized it in that instant, but wrote it off as a hallucination, incorrect interpretation, gap in judgment, or falsified the experience in some other way.

I once knew a financial planner named Alan who admitted to seeing the apparition of his cousin Mark floating in the air at 2:31 am. Mark said that he had just left his physical body and wanted to say goodbye.

Alan was shaken up and went to take a shower. He went back to sleep, and upon waking, was told by his aunt that Mark had died the morning prior, sometime between 2 and 3 am. When Alan checked his watch, it had mysteriously stopped functioning, locked on the time 2:31 am.

However, when questioned about the story, Alan would sometimes speak as if it were true, and sometimes dispute the occasion as having occurred in a dream, and attributed the watch's stopping as mere coincidence.

If Alan were more advanced and had trained as a medium, he would have had the experience to discern the truth of his visitation accurately—and likely communicate with Mark to ask about it.

The majority of the population is a "Magical Maybe." People who fall into this category may have received energy healings in the past, or turned to a spiritual healer when desperate, or studied modern Wicca when they were teenagers. However, except for rare moments of extreme need where they pray because there's nothing else they feel they can do, most of these individuals are open to the idea of Magic, but it isn't integrated into their lifestyle. They may own several crystals and might talk about astrological signs, and may even have a meditation practice, but usually, see spirituality as a valuable but non-critical element of life.

Because of the Kali Yuga (Magical Dark Ages), our bell curve is not even, like the blank image above. Rather, the number of Capable and Advanced Magicians in the Accelerated Growth path is rising, very slightly, every day.

With the end of the Kali Yuga in 2012 and Ascension into the Dwapara Yuga (upward movement of human consciousness), both the Hindu and Mayan calendars agree we are shifting into a Magical Golden Age.

However, that Golden Age just reflects an energetic potential. It is up to us, humans possessing free will, to actualize that potential with our actions and life paths.

Just as we are in an age of extremely advanced technological progress and capability, the same is true for the Magical Sciences.

Group demonstrations of Flashy Magic will help shift this curve. If you participate in a successful endeavor, one powerful memory could elevate your faith, cement your knowledge, and shift you from Capable Magician to Accelerated Growth. Perhaps, if you are the recipient of healing or intentional energies in a Magical experiment, you could even be catapulted into the Advanced category.

It has been known for some gurus to provide energy through the phenomenon of Shaktipat to devotees. This can manifest in the recipient as an activation, transmission, initiation or healing. David has received Shaktipat from both Babaji and Thoth, and many others he is not currently conscious of, in this and other incarnations.

Group Shaktipat is something to augment this type of action and scale it to provide access to many more beings. Shaktipat is traditionally a form of transmission that only occurs with divine grace; it is not something to be scheduled or purchased.

However, the conditions for one being to merit Shaktipat can be intentionally created. They can make it more likely, and while Karma is an ultimate deciding factor, it can be seen and altered by a being with a high enough awareness. Often the practice of atonement (at-one-ment, rebecoming oneness, wholeness) is recommended to change one's karma. In the Roman Catholic tradition, this is known as the process of Absolution.

Consider how could your life change if the ancient techniques were combined with the modern models of sports medicine, where innovations in technology and bodywork have helped athletes recover from injury and accelerate their physical development extremely rapidly.

We want to Grow Up as we Wake Up and ensure maturity of the psychology and ego. Even the most compassionate and intelligent people must undergo a lot of training to reach high levels of spiritual practice. With a combination of well researched Open Sourced Magic, refined and safely performed Magical Experiments, and amplification provided by group intention, we could build institutes for accelerated Magical development.

9. **Unity of Magical Traditions:**

   Let's bring together the peoples of many faiths, uniting a group of Magicians, saints, soothsayers, shamans, witches, druids, Kahunas, Faith healers, Medicine Women, Wise Men, energy healers, Kabbalists, Christian Scientists, Sufis, Qigong healers, and build a global network.

To build an interconnected world, we must see that, while the methods and philosophies vary, we share collective goals for peace, prosperity, harmony, abundance and Love.

How many of our religious and cultural differences actually matter? How many were the result of political systems designed to control people? Instead of focusing on the divisive trends of nationalism, superstition and religious wars, let's focus on our commonalities, and see how we can work together.

Let's use our brains and understand these traditions for what they are. We're mature enough to know that often, throughout time, propaganda and persecution can distort the truth. One need only look at the same news story from liberal, conservative, and multinational perspectives to see that we all view things differently.

By taking a scientific approach to Magic and Mysticism, we can cut through the scary mythology and superficial stereotypes. We can see practitioners for who they truly are, evaluating their deeds and personalities independently from centuries-old generalizations that no longer apply.

And most of all, we can learn to help each other.

Every sincerely dedicated student will find God in the way that is truest for them. This is how Unity is expressed. Not in Uniformity, but in acknowledgment that in all of our variety, we are all one.

A human being has feet, hands, eyes, kidneys and about 5 million hair follicles. Each element is unique, and all work together to create your body. If we were going for uniformity, like those, who say "All must follow our religion or suffer," we would be rotating balls of feet like a freak of nature from Rick and Morty.

More groundedly, we can look at a statement by Pope Francis. He said "Hell is wanting to be distant from God because I do not want God's Love."

Whatever your conception of God, even if you are an atheist and prefer the words Source or Universe, you know what Love is. Since God traditionally means the Source of All Things, we can interpret this quote as defining hell in a way that simply means "turning away from creation" and only seeing destruction, negativity and fear.

It's time for the fear-based proselytizing to end. The truth that exists in the sincerity of your heart is what matters most. The name you use for that truth, and especially the names others use, matter far less than your connection to your higher self, and your connection to the divine.

10. Building Atlantis Reborn:

> I've been blessed with the ability to channel many things, from instructions on how to reactivate mystical abilities, design physical spaces to completely embody any chosen energy as a microcosmic world, and most significantly, I've been given blueprints for Atlantis reborn, a 10 million person city of advanced spiritual and material technologies.

The intended founding date is September 1st, 2041. The city's location is to be located in the Middle East, a critical area in need of a vortex of light to balance the energies of the region and support its restoration to lasting peace, stability, and abundance.

Other details like how the city will thrive economically are known but are not karmically appropriate to share with the general public as of yet. Certain private students and donors will be told as their work harmonizes with some of the ways Atlantis Reborn will affect the world. As of now, we wish to respect the large institutions and legions of jobs that will change as a matter of course in coming decades, as the energy industry adapts to shifts in culture, climate, and technology.

The next Atlantis will provide havens for spiritual groups. Sacred forests where you could experience a full natural immersion. **Massive crystalline and Magical arrays for coalescing energies of healing and manifestation.** Centers for intergalactic culture, where the most trusted sources in the fields of Disclosure can gather to share information as the human race and galactic peoples are ready for it.

Atlantean outposts will also be offered for construction in major cities around the world. There are certain grand scale feats of Magic that require large, complex devices to activate; as we tackle challenges like extreme weather, these devices best serve us by being spread out globally.

These devices, like the Selfic Cabins of Damanhur and Pyramids of Egypt, will have many functions that should be transparent to the world and constructed with multiple safeguards. If there are other large-scale incidents that require an immediate response—say the release of a rogue AI or production of a biohazard in a lab with 3D printers—then powerful Magical devices could play a crucial role in protecting us.

In other ways, large Magical structures and Selfic Cabins can help us achieve deeper states of meditation. What if the effects of the God Helmet, invented by Stanley Koren and developed by neuroscientist Michael Persinger, could be provided to hundreds of people at once? Our trances could deepen, our brains could balance, and our experience of complete and total bliss could be activated with the turn of a switch.

The purpose of such devices aren't to replace our human efforts, but to augment them. It would be wonderful if every student could learn in the presence of a master. With the support of cognitive technologies like the brain sensing Muse headband (found at ChooseMuse.com), we are now able to rate and assess our meditative proficiency.

How do you know how well your training is going without feedback? If you don't have a live human being with you, can technology support you in ways you likely couldn't support yourself?

The original Atlantis was a technologically advanced city. While much of it has been hidden from our memory and historical records based on how the city was destroyed, the core principles remain: Take the best ideas our minds have manifested into form, and provide these forms (devices) as tools to accelerate and augment spiritual development.

We can divinize matter. We can see the Goddess in all things. By mindfully using technologies to understand what's happening in the brain when we enter mystical states, we can have better, more exacting language, and clearer instructions.

Psychological treatments could also evolve to provide Magical support. As "Science, most people don't understand yet," to many people, sound healing, magnetic stimulation of the brain, and the safe and legal use of psychedelics is "Magic."

As our education grows, the word changes. And while we can still use Magic for fun, we're really talking about the Science of Applied Consciousness.

To progress in building Atlantis Reborn, the following support is needed:

- Receivers for transmissions. This requires the use of a professional studio, to receive and the audio and video channelings in a high-quality format.
- Architects, designers, artists, city planners, and engineers to illustrate plans for buildings, temples, laboratories, and housing developments.
- Fundraisers, patrons and donors.
- Support of those who have built, are building and have researched the success and failure of new cities and intentional communities.
- Project managers and administrative assistants
- Researchers on the other Atlantean supporters around the world. There are other beings with similar ideas who have achieved various levels of traction. Wherever possible, it would be ideal to collaborate rather than compete. As this **endeavor is entirely dedicated to the service of humanity,** our approach is people over profit.

11. **An Integrative Model of Divine Sciences, and Building of Temples:**
    Divinities grow more powerful the more we believe in them, and Lakshmi is no exception. The extremely powerful and potent Goddess of Wealth, Lakshmi

supports the material and spiritual success of her followers.

As one of many divinities, Lakshmi offers herself to be both a model for illustrating this concept and recipient of a temple to be constructed.

Wealth and abundance come in all forms, and financial inequality is becoming more transparent as the majority of mainstream currency has become concentrated in fewer individuals in recent decades.

Even with the launch of Cryptocurrency, many people are in debt and believe they are unable to live their purpose until this is resolved fully. How many beings can you think of who, instead of thriving and contributing to the world as aligned with their highest selves, are working a basic wage job as an employee, barely supporting themselves and their Loved ones?

The philosophy offered here is that many divine beings can be compared to thought leaders or community heroes—just orders of magnitude more powerful in the subtle planes. You can follow many humans on Twitter and Facebook, giving acknowledgment and validity to their work, and receive support, advice, and inspiration in return.

Gods and Goddesses are similar. By acknowledging their existence and sharing our Love and admiration, we fuel divinities just as we are fueled by food, water, air, and prana.

Whereas a plant provides oxygen in exchange for carbon dioxide, divine beings often specialize in certain types of energetic relationships. Damanhurian tradition refers to some divine beings as "Machinery" for this purpose. You are free to use that perspective as well as any other.

Consider a massage therapist. If nobody validated his skills, visited or paid him, there's a chance he might not be able to continue in his profession. **The more people who acknowledge his ability, however, the more he is supported to grow, build his education, expand his services, and support many more beings.**

In the short term, this would equate to a full schedule, where he would learn from working on many bodies and see patterns that a less busy might miss. In the long term, a practitioner aligned with helping humanity's spiritual evolution might dedicate some time, funds and community support to open a large clinic, complete with injury rehab, personal training, and services for the poor.

Now consider a being dedicated to a spiritual profession. The 14th Dalai Lama, born Tenzin Gyatso, has been supported by many followers, institutions, patrons, political and cultural leaders, and a rich lineage. Some of the many ways he has contributed to our spiritual growth are:

- Teaching of the Kalachakra Tantra, one of the many teachings of Tibetan Buddhism, to over 200,000 students and disciples at a time
- Publication of 115 books on compassion, happiness, and spirituality as of July 2018
- Advocating for environmental impact, the rights of women, LGBT individuals, and other minorities
- A profoundly deep impact on human beings, often bringing those who interact with him to tears.

The accomplishments and contributions of His Holiness could fill volumes, and we only list these very broad examples to show the relationship between receiving and providing energies. Between moral support, volunteer support, money and everything else Tenzin receives, he has been and continues to be able to be of service at a very large scale.

Gyatso has said "We have had a Dalai Lama for almost five centuries" and discussed the rationale behind whether or not he will choose to reincarnate.

Often as we expand in our psychic and clairvoyant awareness, and gain mystical sight, we also become aware of our past lives, and the greater truth of our immortal soul.

Now imagine a being who has elevated to a level where she has existed as the same ego and name, recognized, prayed to, and supported for hundreds if not thousands of years. During that time, many people report her offering them blessings, transmissions, visions, and healings.

Ascended masters like Jesus, Buddha, Confucius, Mother Mary, Metatron, Melchizedek, Kwan Yin and many others have achieved full Self Realization and served humanity outside of the cycle of death and rebirth. They have shifted to a frequency of light and can materialize bodies anywhere, anytime, at will.

Connecting with the infinite Source, Universe or All that Is can be an abstract concept. When we shift to focus on a specific part of the All and give it human traits, it becomes more relatable.

Some individuals just choose one visage and call it Jesus, or Shiva. Still, others recognize that, while at 9th dimensional Unity we are all one, duality exists simultaneously.

Given this, recognizing an aspect of the All that represents Abundance and Material Success is a simple shift in perspective. **Because we create our reality, if you believe a God or Goddess does or doesn't exist, deep down, your belief will shape your experience.**

Thus, a divine being is also a Permission Slip. Until you claim your full divinity and embody it to the degree of an ascended master, there are beings who can demonstrate more spiritual power than you, just like Olympic weightlifters can bench press more weight than the average person can.

When we connect with the aspect of All that is Lakshmi, we can fuel her with reverence.

Collectively, throughout space and time, we build the frequency, vibration, and the strength of this being in the fields of consciousness. Each of us has a field, which you can for simplicity call an aura. Households have fields, offices have fields; any gathering of minds, plants, crystals or intentions will produce and often strengthen a field.

A room can have a field, giving off good or bad vibes based on what happened in it. So can a forest; so can a concept.

Tapping into the rich field of Abundance that Lakshmi provides is an opportunity to entrain, or link states of consciousness. This leads to the possibility of a richer, deeper and more significant relationship, enabling her to give more and us to receive more... and of course, recognize with clear perceptions her hand in our lives.

The same is true for any aspect of the divine under any name. And, since every element of creation is holographically present in every other element, this concept can apply to human beings as well. When you offer someone respect and support, they are more likely to appreciate and support you in turn.

Because we have chosen to incarnate in a world where money is such a driving force for the conditions of our lives, influencing our health, happiness, and choices, it is both logical and practical to ensure we can flourish financially as well as spiritually.

While it is true that living without money based on donations, gifts and social support is attractive to some, at the time of this writing, our human civilization generally revolves around the exchange of energy known as money.

Healing our individual relationships with wealth, clearing financial traumas, learning to earn more, save more, and achieve our intentions with less money is an extremely worthwhile pursuit, both on the individual and organizational levels.

JK Rowling, the creator of Harry Potter, told Oprah that money frees you, and is "...like a superpower. The luxury of being able to sit down and... not be in any way limited."

Much spiritual and artistic literature avoids or even demonizes the concept of money and those who are good at wielding it. Often, words like Abundance are used to avoid being specific, to the detriment of clarity and being groundedly real with ourselves.

Just like Witches used to be demonized and burned at stake, many movies villainize successful business people. We know logically that intent and results matter more, and so have started to shift this trend, as seen in the brilliant movie Incredibles 2.

If we want to organize effectively and make a significant impact in the world, we must respect the professions and methods that have traditionally been effective at changing it.

If we want to receive respect in turn, we must also forgive those we believe wronged us, and educate ourselves in their vocabulary. This will bring harmony between the traditionally isolated material and spiritual worlds, and unite them as we are learning to unite and equally revere men and women, gay and straight, east and west.

Working with the divine, and in this case, Lakshmi, can free so many of us to do our spiritual and creative work without hindrance, interruption or distraction. While a case can be made that those things can shape us and give us strength, this can also be called justification for avoidance.

The left brain exists. It has unique and important functions. In its analytical and linear abilities, it need not be seen with preference or scorn compared to the creative traits of the right brain.

A harmony between genders. A harmony between nations. A harmony between sides of the brain.

Unity.

We can manifest *anything*, and manifestation does include the requirement of physical action. We live in a world of form, and must respect and include it in our model of reality. We must understand and ideally master the medium through which energy translates into the giving, receiving, and transmutation of form.

Even Esther Hicks, a transmitter of Abraham's Law of Attraction series, started out giving talks in hotel rooms before she filled cruises full of students. Her book *Money and the Law of Attraction* had 539 Amazon reviews as of August 10, 2018; her cornerstone *Law of Attraction* book had 949.

Using this one metric, while not all encompassing, shows that over 56% of her primary audience cares enough about the frequency of energy known as money that they want to study it.

In addition to studying it, the **Temple of Lakshmi** we shall:

- Provide frequent money rituals. I have already offered several and continue to represent Lakshmi and offer her gifts in aligned settings
- Offer training in a wide variety of professional skills
- Provide practical courses on debt resolution and wealth management
- Offer money Magic workshops to help visitors identify, heal and overcome traumas related to money and debt
- Provide free and affordable housing to those dedicated to spiritual service
- Create jobs, grants, internships, and community loan projects
- House research space for alternative, sustainable and post-monetary communities.

And of course, the Temple will support Lakshmi herself and help her serve us in clearing the energies of debt on personal and national scales. At a significant stage, **this could help our leaders and politicians stop trading "favors" with special interest groups, and dedicate more of their time to public service with transparency.**

TEMPLE OF APHRODITE

Love. We seek it. We appreciate it. We substitute it for so many things outside of ourselves: food, pleasurable but unfulfilling relationships, the satisfaction of desires for short-term relief.

True Love is boundless. It is not anchored to any person, place or thing. It is unconditional, literally needing no condition to exist. When you walk into a relationship full of Love, you arrive abundantly, offering, giving, and co-creating. When you walk into a relationship or setting without Love, you come in as needy, sometimes clingy, aiming to "fill the hole in your soul with dope," as Marilyn Manson put it—whatever that dope is for you (mindless sex, drugs, entertainment).

Capitalizing the spelling of the word Love is an act of respect, of reverence. Just as capitalizing the spelling of the word Magic provides a subtle and distinct choice of meaning over stage illusions and fantasy, capitalizing the word Love when we write it helps us focus on the rich, nourishing, unconditional essence of life.

Love is not simply pleasure. It is not a mix of oxytocin and serotonin, though it is often expressed, in part, through these biological markers.

Love transforms. Love can be sent and received through the heart chakra, and Love can be felt through psychic communication as much as it can be offered in touch, words, and eye contact.

SEE YOURSELF, LOVE YOURSELF EXERCISE

The next time you're in front of a mirror, practice gazing into your own eyes with Love. Even if this feels awkward at first, shift your attention from anything your mind speaks, and quietly offer compassionate, unconditional, all-encompassing Love.

Do not label it. Do not place requirements on it. You may set a timer for 3 minutes, to help your mind relax and focus with totality on allowing this spiritual energy to flow forth.

Offer it. Receive it. Feel the truth of Love in abundance.

It requires nothing. Your attention amplifies it, but in feeling it, you recognize its eternal availability, its eternal presence.

As you proceed, notice without intending or changing your intentions how your face shifts. Be the witness in the physical, while existing in the astral-energetic space of pure emotion.

Do this now.

The above exercise should be practiced by all dedicated students at least once per day. If you want to become one of those people who walk around with an aura of peacefulness, stillness, and compassion, focus on the feeling of Love outside of specific circumstances like staring into a mirror. Generate the feeling inside of you and project it outwards, surrounding you in all directions.

LOVING EYE GAZING EXERCISE

Find one person you are close to, open with. Share this idea with them, offering to co-create an experience where you two simply have uninterrupted eye contact.

Before beginning, clean your eyes, and find a comfortable posture. Set a timer, so you don't have to wonder if it's been enough time. Allow your face to relax; don't seek to please or to obtain. You can hold a soft smile, or allow any emotions that naturally arise to express themselves. Just practice being with your partner. Not doing, just being.

This may be the richest connection you have all day.

Once you experience this connection—really a re-connection of our humanity, consider making it a daily practice. Bring it up with anyone who you feel would receive it with kindness. Like a perfect hug, this exercise is meant to be platonic, coming from alignment. It should not be used with any intention other than existing in the shared space of Love, of mutual human support.

Once you become proficient in feeling the energies of Love, you'll see that eye contact is just another permission slip. You'll realize that you can generate this feeling of Love at will.

Do so now. Offer it to someone you've been thinking about, regardless of how they have been treating you.

Next time you see one and can pause for 30 seconds, offer it to a plant. Offer it, without pause or condition, to a barking dog. When walking around the neighborhood, if a dog is barking anxiously or angrily in a constant succession of *yip, yip yip* I simply smile and warmheartedly send her a nourishing stream of Love.

I envision cuddling her, stroking her head. Staring into her eyes, and seeing her calm down. And usually within seconds, she does.

You can practice sending Love to those you care about, and truly any being in your reality. A crying baby. Arguing strangers. Distant friends.

What would it be like to live in Love?

To walk in Love?

To pause, on a regular basis, and refill yourself with Love?

Consider for a moment the following thought experiment.

During the day, count an average number of times you use the restroom.

Compare that to the number of times you pause and take care of your spiritual body, as you are caring for your physical body.

As you take a moment to be in privacy, extend that moment by one minute. Use that minute to fill yourself with Loving, nourishing energies. Tie these activities together so you need not think, or set up more notifications on your phone that can often get ignored in a digital cloud.

Make this very real. Make it part of your life.

Make Love... a priority.

Sometimes our rational mind wants a reason to do things, and when we're particularly in left-brained (or amygdala) mode, focusing just on what needs to happen next, we don't always have the expanded awareness to consider how and who we are for the rest of the day, the week, the month.

During those times, when you're honoring the perfectly valid, equally beautiful aspect of yourself that cares about measuring, and about accomplishments, here's another way to add more Love into your life that doesn't require specific behaviors from other people, and thus can be done by almost any of us, at almost any time or phase of life:

A cool Magical experiment to **observe the effects of Love on the physical world**:

LOVE AS NOURISHMENT EXERCISE

1. Acquire two identical potted plants
2. Get a journal, ideally pen and paper, to put near the pots
3. Treat them physically exactly the same. Measure the amount of water they each receive, and ensure they get equal sunlight.
4. Measure both plants.
5. Every day, for 5 minutes on a timer, send rich, nourishing Love to plant A while plant B is in another location. Do not send Love to plant B.

6. Every week, measure both plants.

7. Repeat for two months. If one plant has shown significantly more growth than the other, share your findings and photos.

I won't prime your subconscious with specific expectations. I simply offer this exercise to the more hard core scientists among you. While results may vary, a sincere effort by anyone who can truly feel the nourishing effects of Love should produce a difference.

If your mind is more achievement oriented and you otherwise don't feel motivated by the first two exercises, re-consider revisiting them after doing the plant exercise, especially the first exercise where you give Love to yourself.

Many spiritual books talk about Love in abstract terms. They are poetic, right-brained, and if you're not in a Lovey state, these texts often don't land. They sound like nice ideas, but especially if you've been suffering or thinking about a recent break-up, they can even be triggering.

They are beautiful, and if you seek them, read books by Kahlil Gibran, Rumi and Marianne Williamson. These authors have all different relationships with Love and express it in deep, heart-centered ways.

To honor the integration of our spirits and our brains, again, a left-brained approach to Love, so that it can be welcomed in *all* of our experiences...not just when we're *feeling* like it.

The ego-mind, the reactive self *wanting* to grow, may especially like this next part.

Those of you who live more from the head than the heart may appreciate this next part (perhaps along with the plant exercise) as well.

A good healer meets his healee where the healee is at. If the healee is experiencing intense emotion, the healer should be aware of, and tune into, that emotion.

If the healee, client or student is coming from a place of immaturity, likely s/he will resonate more with a healer who can speak with the level of vocabulary, complexity, and mental states that are on the level of the recipient.

Keep that in mind, all of you who are heart-centered and are reading this, and feeling distant as we include the words *measurement* and *intention* with Love. This doesn't make the Love insincere. It simply includes *all* of humanity, and allows every reader to have more of a reason to more deeply contemplate, experience and generate Love, *wherever they are at.*

And, as with some of the earlier exercises of this book, allows you to see your own triggers...and Love them as you integrate them.

(The All is in All.)

LOVE ASSESSMENT

We all have different primary use and purpose for Love. Some of us are just more aware of this, and honest with ourselves about it. If we want to change the world in specific ways—say to reduce the amount of suffering in a measurable way, and compare the effectiveness of different methods—we should take the same approach to Love as we do to diet and exercise.

How healthy are you, in a Love sense?

How much Love do you feel on a daily basis?

How Loving are your relationships, to yourself, your body, and other beings?

How quickly can you shift to the frequency of Love in any situation, especially when you catch yourself in moments of stress, frustration or sadness?

Are you open to meditating on the pure essence of Love? Can you deepen the feeling to the point of tears, and expand your field to a certain radius? A sphere 50 feet in diameter, 100, 500?

Can you hold this Love for more than 10 minutes consistently? How about 20?

Can you imagine holding that frequency for even longer, until you can walk in Love, feeling the blissfulness of being taken care of and exuding abundance in your attitude as a way of life?

How is it practical for you to make a plan, set a goal, to experience more Love in your life?

If it is even the least bit practical, pause now and invest 10 minutes to create certain goals around Love.

Perhaps you will practice the above exercises daily for 30 days and journal your experience. Perhaps you will seek to add a loving connection with another human being, and see them for two hours every weekend. Perhaps you will think of the person who drains you of loving energy, and reduce your time with them by 50%.

As you brainstorm several goals, before you finish the exercise, commit to one of them. Schedule it in your calendar for a time and setting that feels easy to honor. Set up some structure in your life, some unique reminder, to support this goal in manifesting.

Do so now.

This writing is designed for the left-brained, divine masculine, logical self because those of us who experience logically-dominated states may seek *reasons* for Love.

We are here to serve, and to bring balance between the spiritual and material worlds.

We must be able to Love all, including the richly emotional and the richly logical.

We must shift to see everything as an expression of the divine, and seek to be whole-brained beings, instead of simply existing in what is dominant, comfortable and habitual.

As one of the many Goddesses of Love, Aphrodite's presence is much needed in these times. We could all use a boost of Loving presence at home while traveling, and especially in the workplace.

All of our interactions could benefit from a richer, more consistent Love field, from parent-child relationships to simple transactions at the grocery store or coffee shop.

What we send, we receive.

Building a temple to Aphrodite is building a temple dedicated to expanding our awareness, proficiency, and ability to Love. As an aspect of the infinite divine anthropomorphized into a being we can conceive of in ways we're used to (face, name, body), Aphrodite is one of the many aspects of Love to which we can relate.

Countless other beings, like Jesus, Krishna, Yogananda, and Gaia will be depicted in Aphrodite's temple. Love is universal and has no single face.

For the conventions of culture, we need a specific name and a recognizable vocabulary. As with the temples of Lakshmi and Thoth, consider in your heart, and support us if you feel so called, to acknowledge the many aspects of Love and how it materializes, and both the concrete and the abstract.

As with all divinities, a tribute to Aphrodite acknowledging her existence is both in service to her and an enabler to receive her support. Just as there are Love specialists in the fields of psychology, marriage counseling, and artistic expression,

Aphrodite can be considered a Love expert in the seventh-dimensional divine realm, where many beings focus on many aspects of creation.

Based on the culture of humanity at the time of this writing, some of the offerings of this temple will be:

- Classes to understand the many faces of the divine, and build our vocabulary of other known divine beings who represent Love, to build tolerance and support for international collaboration independent of specific words and representations

- Talks on how the frequency of Love can heal humans, animals and plants

- Meditations and rituals to build very strong fields of Love. These will be extremely nourishing to all participants, and we will offer concentrated and focused energies of Love to those in need of healing across our world, and other worlds.

- Workshops and spaces for a healthy, Loving and compassionate touch, based on the comfort and consent of each individual. Both nonsexual and sexual spaces will exist based on community interest and professional support.

- On-site testing and treatment for infectious diseases and STIs

- Grounded, thorough, mature, compassionate and uncensored education on many sexual topics, including technique, connection to yourself and your partner, self-Love, and with sexual practices of the Kama Sutra and Tantric traditions. The services offered will depend on local laws, and we will have a database of trusted and accredited practitioners in other regions who can offer additional services in safe, Loving, compassionate sexual experiences that are centered on spiritual development.

- Education and training in the transmutation and mastery of sexual energies. This training will combine many effective traditions that are known to improve health, performance, and stamina.

- Space and support for a community of beings who wish to remain celibate, both for those who wish to not engage with sexual acts with other beings and who wish for a life of no physical sexual activity in general.
- A safe space and living quarters for beings who are recovering from sexual trauma, abuse, and human trafficking
- Supportive services for LGBT individuals, beings who feel aligned with non-binary genders, and those who are seeking experienced, compassionate mentorship related to their sexuality
- Matchmaking services for those seeking a Loving person in their lives, whether this person is a romantic partner or an adopted brother, sister, mother, father, son, daughter, friend or mentor.
- Relational healing services for all of the previous categories.

The Temple of Aphrodite, along with other temples, will comprise of a flagship space, a complex of buildings that can support over 10,000 souls at a time. Over time, satellite temples will be built, existing in locations that appreciate them, offering services desired by the local community and being respective of local communities.

THE TEMPLE OF THOTH

Thoth, God of Magic in the Egyptian tradition and author of the Emerald Tablets, shares an incarnation with the Greek god Hermes Trismegistus, author of the *Hermetic Corpus*, a series of sacred texts that are a basis for Hermeticism.

Thoth-Hermes is often combined in reference as a patron of alchemy and astrology. For simplicity and focus, we use the name Thoth.

You may view Thoth as an ascended master, a powerfully evolved time traveling human, alien, or God. Ultimately, beings who ascend (as with the story of Thoth's ascent in the Emerald Tablets) are elevated to great levels because their spiritual status is inconceivable to most mortals of everyday consciousness.

For a good illustration of this concept, see the clip *Flatland* from *What The Bleep do We Know*. It shows how higher dimensional beings appear as Gods to lower dimensional beings in a very grounded and funny animation, and as of this writing can be found at https://www.youtube.com/watch?v=BWyTxCsIXE4.

Choose the story that feels right to you. We all have a divine spark inside and are all re-awakening Gods and Goddesses incarnate.

Magic is on the rise. I as David Solomon have worked with, channeled, and partially embodied Thoth. I surrender parts of my ego-mind to him daily, embodying this higher dimensional consciousness that is honoring the call of so many beings to re-embody on this earth, at this time.

Neuroscientist Dr. Thomas Antone observed during neurofeedback that my high beta waves spiked from 7 to 14 millivolts during one of Thoth's transmissions; 14 millivolts is often associated with spikes in psychic phenomena.

Alchemists are scientists, and Magic, as we have said, is the science of applied consciousness. As one of the greatest allies we have in this world, Thoth wants to help our innovations move forward. Just as he inspired (came **in** as **spirit**) notable inventors like Tesla, Thoth is available to be received to all willing and sincere devotees.

A note of caution for the next few paragraphs: Many traditions warn against embodying a spirit "outside of ourselves." If you have legitimately touched, and can return to, Unity consciousness, you know from an embodied perspective that all spirits are elements of you, and cannot harm you.

If for any reason you hold the belief that opening yourself to outside consciousness can also open yourself to beings like demons, imps, and other negative entities, then skip the previous exercises, or perform them while surrounding yourself with white light. If you have training in a tradition that includes psychic protection, you may perform it as well.

You are a being with free will. You are not required to do anything that you feel is not in your highest alignment.

Being a devotee in our system does not necessarily mean a lifetime vow. While it can, and while permanent shifts occur all the time, being a devotee of Thoth is, in any moment of now, **surrendering one's ego completely to embody a frequency of the all that represents itself as a Master of Magic.**

Surrendering the ego means you can be in a room with 11 other advanced spiritual beings who also offer themselves as vessels to Thoth, so we can cross reference and validate channeled transmissions.

Yet when alone, if you wish to receive knowledge from the Akashic Records or collective unconscious, if you want to feel a jolt of chi, an insight or Magical revelation, consider calling on Thoth. He is a being of light and service just as he is an aspect of your higher self, and will come when sincerely called.

If you prefer, you can do this practice instead with the essence of Jesus, or of your higher self. More advanced techniques for spiritual embodiment will be discussed in future books, and guided practices will be provided both in our digital and live workshops of our mystery school.

The openness of your heart, mind, and ego to receive any "higher" aspect of you will determine the degree of your experience, between physical sensation and ideative insights.

In the Temple of Thoth, we will:

- Create, enhance and distribute Magical artifacts, such as wands, staves, charged crystals, jewelry, tinctures and potions, spiritual armor, amulets of psychic protection, and healing tools.

- Provide Magical training to beings of all levels of skill, linked to vows of service to the light and life of the world.

- Discuss the value of a vow as a security measure; just like the right to drive if one promises to drive safely, simple vows of not causing Magical harm will be offered with simple Magical techniques. Since learning to fly a harrier jet involves considerable more power (and risk if abused), more advanced levels of training will come with more safeguards.

- Create Magical experiments, designing, measuring, tracking and innovating different techniques to identify the most effective, efficient and powerful methods for creating significant positive change in our world.

- House Adepts of the Arts, Magical practitioners of many traditions who agree to codes of tolerance, cooperation, and compassionate service to the flourishing of life across the cosmos.

- Offer group meditations supported with a blend of transformative technologies, binaural beats, devices that use light to affect the brain and induce altered natural states, sound healing, ecstatic dance, mantra chanting, martial arts and tea ceremonies.

- Offer services of and training for psychics, mediums, alchemists, druids, birth and death doulas, shamans and other disciplines.

- Hold regular Channeling sessions with groups of people who embody the same being, so we can scientifically and rationally verify the transmissions of nonphysical entities, Gods and Goddesses, Angels and Archangels, and other beings who wish to Lovingly interact with and support humanity's Ascension.

- Examine prophecies of all traditions, and publish regular updates that take into account Mayan and Hindu calendars, astrology, shifts in Earth's magnetic field, Polar activity, greater galactic energies, portals, precognitions, and similar views of our reality from higher-dimensional perspectives that can see through time.

  So much as one can be built, we will build a model that has the highest level of accuracy of seeing into future probable timelines, so information can be shared to increase the probability of desired timelines, and decrease the probability of undesired, disastrous timelines.

- Hold voting councils open to world leaders, powerful scientists and organizations, and representations of citizens, channelers of nature spirits, and all intelligent life. Incorporate these things with prophetic data along with scientific data related to how our choices can shape our future.

- Collect and distribute resources to support the best and most harmonious futures.

- Research and perform, as karmically appropriate and technologically feasible, safe and stable time travel to correct or prevent major events that could significantly destabilize life (nuclear war, genocides, etc.). Damanhur is known as a community that has researched (and possibly performed) time travel, along with several governments.

  Since a successful mission will be fully integrated into the timeline with the "previous timeline" only visible through isolated items like a textbook in a "neutral chamber" that is unaffected from the changes, time travel can be one of the most subtle and powerful ways to affect the world and thus will only be considered with the highest caution.

- Build a model of integrative sciences. If over 95% of the world is "dark matter" and "dark energy" that can't currently be measured, how much of this is actually the astral, angelic and other planes?

As we link the material-reductionist and spiritual-faith worlds, we can consider drawing maps between the unknown and the known. PhDs in quantum physics and string theory will also be welcome to integrate these fields, very often bridges to the Magical Realm.

- Host Magical Olympic Games so we can have fun with heightened abilities, and enjoy them! Can we offer accelerated evolution to plants, so they can dance? Can we figure out how to help dogs communicate telepathically, or grow vocal chords to talk through some highly evolved placebo effect? Can we perfect levitation to the point of flight, and invent an entire category of aerial sports? What else would you try?

The more we engage with divine energies (or consciousness ascended to the Divine level of awareness), the more we are supported in our own paths of self-realization.

When fully realized, we exist at unity awareness and see ourselves as fully complete and indivisible with the divine.

At this state, our egos, our "small selves" have come to know themselves so clearly and Lovingly that there is no longer any inner drama, turmoil or disagreement between dis-integrated components of the self.

We are at one with our intuition, guides, and Oversoul. We may use a persona that has a name and physical appearance, but we know in a fully embodied sense that this is merely a representation of the vastness that we are as infinity itself.

As individual divinities exist primarily on the 7th dimension, and unity refers to the 9th dimension, focusing on talking with, receiving from and embodying divine beings is a stepping stone to a vastly greater reality.

Most of us learn to walk before we can run, but some of us make the leap from crawling on the ground to quickly sprinting across the floor.

If you have an ability to access Unity consciousness, experience self-realization and transcend the supporting structures of egos—be they mortal or divine—then do so, as often as you can.

At full states of Unity, Enlightenment, and Nonduality, there is simultaneously no need for anything to be done, and all needs for all things to be both created and erased.

Those who see only the Light may say "Nothing need be done," yet in considering the totality of existence, we realize there is both darkness and shadow. While contemplating this, until the shadows of your ego are fully Loved, dissolved and integrated, and until your psychic protections are strong, do not fool yourself into justifying harmful actions—even and especially under the guise of "embodiment of a wrathful God."

For these reasons, **it is best to reside in the side of Unity that is Light.**

And while this is by definition duality as it excludes darkness, a safer and more stable dimensional awareness of 8.5 may keep safe and your physical body out of jail, whereas many the delusional mystic has spiritually justified immoral actions with rationalizations based on principles they do not understand.

This is the difference between "Waking Up" and "Growing Up."

If you were fully Awake to your unlimited Divine power but hadn't resolved all the grievances of your childhood and adult life, one day someone could disagree with you... and you could choose to dissolve him into a puddle of goo.

On the other hand, if you have "Grown Up" and are fully mature, it's safer to Wake Up to a wider range of your abilities and see the perfection in all beings. You are less likely to shift into a "Spiritual Ego" and justify satisfying your desires with advanced abilities, just like an emotionally mature wrestling champion doesn't beat up someone who looks at her the wrong way.

If someone spits in your face and you gaze kindly and Lovingly back at him, you will have a far more positive impact on his spiritual development than, say, snapping your fingers and breaking his legs.

Resting in Unity consciousness can be very restorative. It can help you detach from material matters so completely that you erupt in ecstatic laughter at the silliness of life, and the silliness of your ego in wanting certain things to matter so much.

Living in Unity consciousness can also be extremely self-sustaining.

If you are able to maintain it, there is no reason for you to take any actions in the material world, including preserving the vitality of your own body. Even if you know how to master your Chi and survive without food, water or air like Pilot Baba, at some point, you may be presented with the spontaneous opportunity to **take the Bodhisattva Vow** and become a being who seeks to maintain Buddhahood (persistent self-realization) for the benefit of all sentient beings.

In other words, descend from Samadhi and return to duality.

A true Magician is master of both the heavens and the earth. Residing in both simultaneously, we shift from "One who practices Magic" to One who *is* Magic.

One who *is* Source.

One who is Divine.

The path of Magic is like many other paths to enlightenment.

At the center of existence is a lake. All beings end up at the lake to drink. Some walk, some crawl, some fly. Some are carried, some drive, some teleport.

All are Equal in the eyes of the infinite.

The paths go by different names. Judaism. Christianity. Buddhism. Hinduism. Persistent Non-Symbolic Expression. Magical Studies.

Which one will you take?

Which one have you already chosen, and in this moment, perhaps remember?

I cannot say that this road has been easy. While I have memories and perceptions of parallel timelines, I also see and feel every moment of this incarnation.

Two near death experiences, one with my liver, the other with my heart.
Experiencing abuse.

Experiencing ridicule and scorn.

Being called insane.

I've built companies and felt my ego dissolve while in devout prayer. I've visited Jerusalem in Israel and studied in Damanhur. I've felt the rich, tingling energies of Lakshmi and Thoth in my body as I offered transmissions to others and charged physical objects, and felt my awareness shift into psychedelic states without plant medicines or drugs.

I've been offered mystical experiences, materializations, healings, precognitions, and rich connections with beautifully embodied souls. I've experienced so many challenges to burn off karma and ensure that, before this book could be published, I could walk in and embody the Light to a degree commensurate with the responsibility I see.

I have succeeded, I have failed, and I have opened myself up for feedback.

Like you, I am human. I have acted in ways I wish I hadn't, and have asked for forgiveness in allowing my small self to dominate in certain actions.

Like you, I am remembering myself as divine. I have surrendered, and allowed greater Spirit to flow through me. At especially inspired moments, this has led to not just the channeling of words which brought you this book, but the channeling of actions of a precise nature.

A blank canvas is like a blank slate. Who would you become if you had a fresh start? If you could push "reset" on your entire past, on all your bills, all the things you have ever said and have ever been said about you...and could pick a new name, a new location, a new self to purely design and redesign as you saw fit?

Inspiration flows through many channels. One such channel is art.

If you have been experiencing Magic is Real in a visual form, you have seen the paintings. These were channeled, often only the very next action known once the previous action was complete. In a studio with over 400 art supplies, I intuitively selected, applied, blended, altered and harmonized the paint and the canvas while being fully present.

These are portals. They are vehicles for transmission. They are works of beauty...and they are for you.

Of hundreds of paintings, only 13 were selected for this book. If you have been listening or otherwise have a version of this content without the art, you should be able to find it online.

The perfection of a painting is like the perfection of your life. Do you look for flaws, how one color could be brighter, dimmer, wider, smaller? Do you begin a painting as you begin a day, open to all possibilities or feeling dictated by your past actions, the sunk costs?

Do you decide to finish, perhaps build a series of artworks and experiences...or do you put down the brush?

When we see all things as perfect, all previously considered mistakes change to be just another manifestation of Unity as it sought to be expressed in that moment. Nothing need be changed.

Everything is as it should be.

I have remembered, more and more every day, to shift into a state dedicated to serving others, offer healings, and witness miracles as simple as flowers blooming as my face beamed in a radiant smile at the beauty of life, smelling fresh air and feeling the warm rays of sun from a clear sky.

I (as you) smile in this, our co-creation.

I (as you) wish for you what you wish for yourself.

And if your wishes have manifested with our co-creation of this book, and your ego-mind wishes for the experience of the visions outlined as in this chapter, the version of you that is me... David Solomon... could use your support.

Over 1000 more pages of *Magic is Real* have been drafted as of this writing. I as David Solomon have given workshops, talks, healing sessions and trainings. I have taken on apprentices and have studied with over a dozen embodied masters, and many more who reside in the realm of the nonphysical; indeed, this is the realm where lately, I have been learning the most.

But I am only one man.

Even though I have been privileged to share the messages you have received, in order to manifest them, I need you.

You are a part of this world just as much as I. Together, we co-create our consensus reality, the reality that exists in physical form.

While in states of divine awareness, all timelines are seen, and in Unity, all are truly one. At higher dimensions, we are linked, our individuality blurs, and the components of a greater Oversoul that we are part of... like cells in the body of God.

To transition from astral and higher realms are of potentiality, of probability, we must honor the earth as well as the heavens. In this world of form, as we as ego-minds that touch the Divine... as we re-integrate closer to Unity, we must coalesce, combine our efforts, and combine our energies.

To transition from potentiality into actuality, to raise probabilities to the level of embodied 100% truth, we must engage in the practice of manifestation.

If there were enough collective belief for me to materialize a palace in half a second, I would. If there were enough collective belief in me to teleport to you at this moment or appear in some other form, I would, and if your belief were sufficient, you would see me, and we would talk.

Yet this day, the day you encounter this text, our collective belief exists as it is. And thus, as of this first edition of Magic is Real, you have this book, and on this date, physically, not yet a temple—much less three.

Nor have you the city of Atlantis Reborn.

Except in potentiality.

My friend and fellow student, this is an offering for you to co-create with me. For us, as reflections of each other and components of the same greater soul, to manifest visions that can only come to being with the efforts of many minds.

Whatever your state, whatever your means or desires, **you have the power to help actualize this dream.**

You know inside how you can help.

If you see someone as powerful, your thoughts increase their power. If you feel this way toward me, I request your thoughts and your prayers humbly, that I may continue to serve and be protected, offering these Magical transmissions to reawaken the world.

If you feel this way towards me, I offer to you the exercise of co-creation as you sit down daily, for five minutes or more, and visualize the success of these Temples, as outlined above.

Pick one quality, or pick several. Sit for five minutes or five hours. Feel the emotions this vision evokes within you, as you know emotion is key in manifestation. See yourself as existing in the halls of these temples, taking part in the activities, living in a world benefiting from their existence.

Give of yourself, if you feel so called, to this, our co-creation.

And so shall it be.

If you see someone as capable, your time, finances, and social media activity can help spread their message, and help actualize their goals. I offer unto you; **these are not the goals of an ego-mind named David Solomon; they are the goals of collective humanity, channeled through a willing vessel.**

And if you agree, if you agree that we share these goals and that you wish to see your goal actualized, then please, in whatever way that feels aligned, support the manifestation of our shared vision for a more Magical world.

A temple is built brick by brick.

Who will lift the bricks? Who will craft them, transport them? Who will ring the bells, chant the chants, light the incense?

Who will be the organizer of events to help heal Loved ones? Who will be in charge of the technology to both capture and enhance our efforts? Who among you feel called to dedicate himself, herself, or themselves to develop advanced spiritual abilities, and serve humanity as an Awakened Magician so that we can shift into the next Golden Age?

The choice is yours.

There are infinite timelines to experience. There are infinite universes to shift into. Your actions, physical and nonphysical, shape these realities for you and other beings, especially those who do not fully realize and claim their true power.

With enough of us holding hands, we could materialize that temple. Whether it takes half a second or half a century depends on our conviction, and our faith.

And our actions.

I have stepped away from lucrative careers in business and finance. I have dedicated myself to full and complete spiritual service, and have seen the future timelines in which I may serve. I invite you, here, today, now, to experience the timeline where our visions, above, are collectively manifest.

Not just in idea, but in form.

Will you join me? Have you already?

Your answer, whatever it is, in the truest depths of your heart of hearts, is perfect.

I honor it, and I honor you.

And I thank you, most profoundly, for your time.

Blessed be, in love and light,

-David Solomon

Acknowledgements

To all of you cherished friends, teachers, family members, spirit guides, past and parallel selves, divine supporters, chimeras, familiars, angels, spirits, and, especially *you*, fellow students of the Arts!

I send you immense gratitude for this work.

Magic is Real is here because of you have chosen to support the restoration of our civilization's lost Magical knowledge.

This book is dedicated to you.

Falco Tarrasco, Founder of Damanhur

Together, we form a collective. Our group intention shapes everything of our physical reality, from the strength of the Magic we experience to the very weather on Gaia.

All of us are creators. Whether we create intentionally or unconsciously depends on our path. If this book has helped you step into your creative power as a Magician, then pause... and truly feel that all of your gratitude, all of your discoveries and joy...

were, at some level, your manifestation as much as mine. This book is our co-creation.

Acknowledgements go to all of the beings who have been named in these pages. All of the fellow authors, teachers, and students on my path have contributed to journey, each the brick of a grand temple continually expanding in infinite evolution.

Along with many formal teachers, the wider Consciousness community of the San Francisco Bay Area and the global festival communities gave pivotal experiences to make this book possible. To all my friends, my family, and my tribe: thank you for your love and support.

We are always learning. As the Science of Applied Consciousness (or the more fun term, *Magic*) evolves, our understanding, instructions and implications evolve with it.

In his book *Bold*, Peter Diamandis said "The day before something is truly a breakthrough, it's a crazy idea...Trying out crazy ideas means bucking expert opinion and taking big risks."

When I started this project, I was risking a reputation with some very notable Silicon Valley communities, and over a decade of entrepreneurial momentum. Full of successes and failures, my business life and intellect took me far...and in that experience we so often have with the stories that touch us, like Dr Strange, I reached a point where my intellect could take me no further.

At some point, I released my fear of failing. Through a mix of receiving healing sessions and allowing my soul to embody at greater levels, I realized that "failure" in the superficial sense might occur again, in small or large ways.

With all the determination and alignment I felt, I also knew that the universe could throw obstacles in my path, including ones that looked like failure, to offer opportunities to embrace humility (of which many more are coming, for all of us!) and surrender. As Dr. Diamandis continued, "The road to bold is paved with failure, and this means having a strategy in place to handle risk and learn from mistakes is critical."

That strategy is our tribe. This book is your invitation to join it.

Thus, if I am ever shown to be incorrect, and a greater truth is more clearly and accurately expressed, I have included a space for such to be known in the safe container of an *Open Sourced Magic Wiki* on MagicalGoldenAge.com.

This is for the betterment and growth of all—and let us see the stepping stone that may be called a "failure" be seen as valuable as any success or incremental improvement, be it the original version of the printing press, or your very first mobile device, which, while at the time likely served well, by now has likely undergone many stages of evolution.

While there are many statements in these pages that can be called timeless, this book (and really, most if not all content) is contextual to the culture, era and language in which it arose.

This book is dedicated to all those who stood for their truth, those who knew they were souls and not bodies, and yet while in those bodies, stood for the Truth in all matters. The definition of God is owned by no one, and is infinitely abundant to all.

To my Hasidic brothers, dancing on your way to the chamber... to my Pagan sisters, serving with love, life after life, as wise women helping weave the web of healing and song, in thatched huts with crushed herbs, going back eons and surviving the burning times and more... and to all the First Nations, indigenous peoples who held their honor, their heritage, their marvelous gifts for humanity intact, though their culture and very way of life be challenged, generation after generation, by the hegemonic powers that appear, at long last, to be losing the battle for control over the human race: how we live our lives, and how we know our own truths, collective and individual, as divine beings.

This book is also dedicated, most importantly and specifically, to the process that is Life. While I have the privilege of discussing Unity and Magic with you in a path of divine embodiment, I do acknowledge that we live in a world of form, of biological life, a world of complexity. This book became significantly refined in Damanhur, Italy, where I (re)learned of a more full context of the battle between Dark and Light, Life and Entropy, Complexity and Void.

Damanhur is a community of many Magical researchers and students who have built Temples of Humankind, what many have called the Eighth Wonder of the World. Damanhurian philosophy is based on positive thinking, action, and an understanding that each of us cares to contribute to the evolution of humanity.

Damanhurian schools of Alchemy, Healing and Meditation are very high quality organizations that help remind us of our divine spark, and the harmony that exists between divinities of many traditions around the world.

Special consideration (in no particular order) to David Ray, Lars King, Louison Dumont, Sean Batir, Jeffery Martin, Anna-Lisa Adelberg, Raina Delear, Kristen Greco, Betsy Pool, Debbie and Larry Landau, Mikey Siegel of Consciousness Hacking, Renat Gabitov, Justin Faerman and Jackie Knechtel of the Flow Mastery Institute, Brandon Beachum of Positive Head, Ray Maor, Kathleen Stevens, Lois Pearl, Miriam Weininger, Michael and David Hrostoski, Burgiel, Bashar, Paul Selig, Adam Atman, Adam Curry, Nicky Chirch, Max Marmer, Chris Catterton, Casey Lake, Connor Paschall, Jack Reeder, Ryuho Okawa, Guy Laliberté, Florak, Michael Mazzola, Jeroen de Wit, Joshua Falcon-Grey, Rebecca Getachew, Verenice Berrora, Wisp Way, Goura Loto, Anaconda Papaya, Ragno Lattuga, Falco Tarrasco, Cavaluccio Marino Arnica, Jessica Jacobson, Tursiope, Terrier Ruzzon, Evelyn Hills, James David Wade, Ray Ayer, Benjamin Ayer, Mark Tanaka, John Scalzi, the Center for Applied Rationality in Berkeley, CA, the Center for Positive Organizational Scholarship in Ann Arbor, MI, Brendon Burchard, JK Rowling, Stan Lee, Alan Moore, Oprah Winfrey, Will Smith, Jim Carrey, Scarlett Johansson, Robert Downey Jr, Dean Radin, Sam Neill, Tim Burton, Helena Bonham Carter, Elizabeth Gilbert, Marvin Yagoda, Ralph Williams, Sheryl Sandberg, Tim Ferriss, Robin Williams, Dr. Wayne Dyer, Dr. Martin Luther King Jr., Starhawk, Mantak Chia, Silver RavenWolf, David Hawkins, Richard Feinman, Thoth, Lakshmi, Jesus Christ, Bhagavan Krishna, Mahavatar Babaji, Lahiri Mahasaya, Swami Sri Yukteswar, Paramahansa Yogananda, Arjuna, Amma, Merlin, Gautama Buddha, Horus, Archangel Metatron, Michael Monk of the Avatar Energy Mastery Institute, and those individuals who shall nameless, and all other reflections of Unity: Thank you profoundly. Your contributions to my life, directly and indirectly, have helped me rediscover my divinity and transform, shed and evolve the ego-mind in especially meaningful ways, and have thus enabled what has, and is, to come.

About The Author

David Solomon's purpose is to discover, improve and teach Real Magic by building the best mystery school in the world.

He has experienced over 111 miracles, synchronicities, siddhis, and overt moments of Real Magic. This book has been a major undertaking that has transformed him and seen many revisions as humanity shifts timelines and his own consciousness evolves.

He lives in the San Francisco Bay Area and is grateful to be included in tribes of joyful spiritual people who are devoted to helping humanity thrive in sustainable harmony with Mother Earth.

To request a workshop, talk, or private session, please visit MagicalGoldenAge.com.